AUSTRALIA AND NEW ZEALAND   Political Map

Names of cities over 1,000,000 are capitalized

National capitals   _Canberra_
State capitals   SYDNEY
State Boundaries   Railroads

0   50   100   200   300   400   500 Miles
0   100   200   300   400   500   600   800 Kilometers

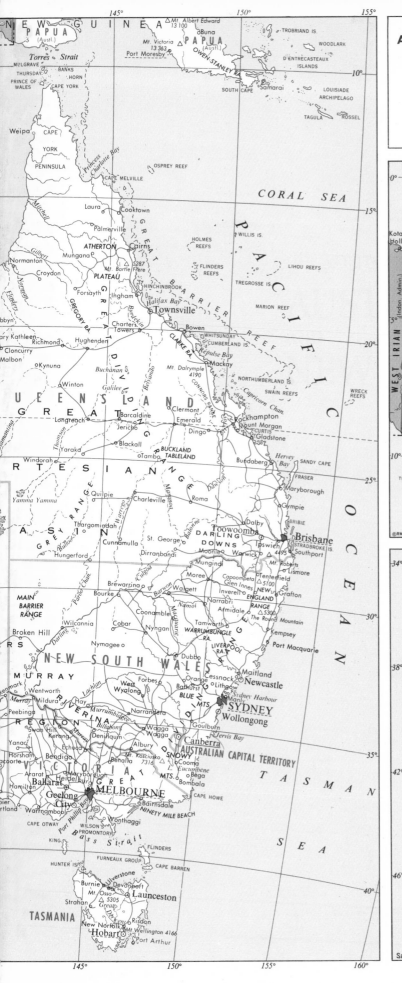

Main Map (Australia)

NEW GUINEA
PAPUA (Austl.)
Torres Strait
MULGRAVE
THURSDAY
PRINCE OF WALES
CAPE YORK
Weipa
CAPE YORK PENINSULA
PENINSULA
Normanton
Croydon
Mungana
ATHERTON PLATEAU
Cairns
Mt. Bartle Frere 5287
Ingham
HINCHINBROOK I.
Halifax Bay
Townsville
Charters Towers
Bowen
WHITSUNDAY IS.
CUMBERLAND IS.
Mackay
Repulse Bay
QUEENSLAND
Mt. Dalrymple 4190
CONNORS RANGE
NORTHUMBERLAND IS.
SWAIN REEFS
Capricorn Chan.
Rockhampton
Mount Morgan
CURTIS
Gladstone
Hervey Bay
SANDY CAPE
FRASER
Bundaberg
Maryborough
Gympie
BRIBIE
STRADBROKE IS.
Brisbane
Ipswich
Southport
Toowoomba
DARLING DOWNS
Warwick
Dalby
Moonie
Lismore
Grafton
NEW ENGLAND RANGE
Armidale
The Round Mountain
Tamworth
WARRUMBUNGLE RA.
Kempsey
Port Macquarie
LIVERPOOL RA.
NEW SOUTH WALES
Dubbo
Orange
Bathurst
Lithgow
Maitland
Newcastle
Cessnock
BLUE MTS.
Sydney Harbour
SYDNEY
Manly
Wollongong
Jervis Bay
Goulburn
Canberra
AUSTRALIAN CAPITAL TERRITORY
SNOWY
Mt. Kosciusko 7316
Cooma
Eucumbene
GREAT
Bombala
CAPE HOWE
TASMAN SEA
NINETY MILE BEACH
Bairnsdale
WILSON PROMONTORY
Bass Strait
FLINDERS
FURNEAUX GROUP
CAPE BARREN
HUNTER IS.
Ulverstone
Burnie
Devonport
Mt. Ossa 5305
Launceston
Strahan
TASMANIA
New Norfolk
Mt. Wellington 4166
Hobart
Port Arthur
VICTORIA
Ballarat
Geelong City
MELBOURNE
Heidelberg
Maryborough
Bendigo
Echuca
Swan Hill
Mildura
Wentworth
MURRAY
RIVERINA
REGION
Albury
Wagga Wagga
Narrandera
Hay
Deniliquin
Wangaratta
MAIN BARRIER RANGE
Broken Hill
Wilcannia
Cobar
Nyngan
Bourke
Brewarrina
Walgett
Narrabri
Moree
Mungindi
Inverell
Glen Innes
Tenterfield
Grafton
GREAT DIVIDING RANGE
Roma
Charleville
Quilpie
Cunnamulla
Thargomindah
Hungerford
St. George
Dirranbandi
Longreach
Barcaldine
Jericho
Blackall
Tambo
BUCKLAND TABLELAND
Emerald
Dingo
Clermont
Winton
Yaraka
Windorah
Yamma Yamma
Barcoo
Thomson
Laura
Cooktown
Palmerville
CAPE MELVILLE
Princess Charlotte Bay
OSPREY REEF
CORAL SEA
PACIFIC OCEAN
GREAT BARRIER REEF
HOLMES REEFS
WILLIS IS.
FLINDERS REEFS
TREGROSSE IS.
LIHOU REEFS
MARION REEF
WRECK REEFS
Cloncurry
Malbon
Kynuna
Richmond
Hughenden
Winton
Kathleen
Mt. Albert Edward 13 100
Mt. Victoria 13 363
Port Moresby
OWEN STANLEY RA.
Buna
TROBRIAND IS.
WOODLARK
D'ENTRECASTEAUX ISLANDS
Samarai
SOUTH CAPE
LOUISIADE ARCHIPELAGO
TAGULA
ROSSEL
BANKS
HORN

Inset 1 (New Guinea)

PACIFIC   OCEAN
Equator
NINGO IS.
HERMIT IS.
ADMIRALTY IS.
MUSSAU
EMIRAU
MANUS
NEW HANOVER
Kavieng
BISMARCK
NEW IRELAND
Namatanai
Rabaul
Kokopo
ARCH.
Kotabaru
Hollandia
Humboldt-Baai
Aitape
Wewak
Sepik
TERRITORY OF NEW GUINEA
(AUSTRALIAN TRUSTEESHIP)
WEST IRIAN (Indon. Admin.)
NEW GUINEA
PAPUA (AUSTRALIA)
BISMARCK RA.
RAMU
Madang
KARKAR
LONG
Talasea
VITU IS.
NEW BRITAIN
The Father 7546
Strickland
Mt. Wilhelm 15 400
Mt. Giluwe 13 660
Mt. Bangeta 13 454
Lae
Salamaua
Huon Gulf
BOUGAINVILLE
TRENCH
Morobe
13 100
Fly
Gulf of Papua
Mt. Albert Edward 13 100
DARU
Port Moresby
OWEN STANLEY RA.
Mt. Victoria 13 363
Buna
TROBRIAND IS.
WOODLARK
D'ENTRECASTEAUX IS.
Samarai
Torres Strait
THURSDAY
CAPE YORK
CAPE YORK PENINSULA
GREAT BARRIER REEF
CORAL SEA
Same scale as main map

Inset 2 (New Zealand)

CAPE REINGA
NORTH CAPE
Kaitaia
Bay of Islands
Russell
PACIFIC OCEAN
Devonport
GREAT BARRIER ISLAND
Hauraki Gulf
Auckland
Manukau
NORTH ISLAND
Hamilton
Bay of Plenty
EAST CAPE
North Taranaki Bight
New Plymouth
C. EGMONT
Mt. Egmont 8260
South Taranaki Bight
Rotorua
Whakarewarewa
Lake Taupo
Waitara
TONGARIRO NAT. PARK
Ruapehu 9175
Wanganui
Napier
Hawke Bay
Hastings
Gisborne
Palmerston North
Wellington
Lower Hutt
CAPE FAREWELL
Tasman Bay
Nelson
Karamea Bight
CAPE FOULWIND
Greymouth
Hokitika
SOUTH ISLAND
SOUTHERN ALPS
FRANZ JOSEF GLACIER
Mt. Cook 12 349
CASCADE PT.
Milford Sd.
Te Anau
Wakatipu
RESOLUTION ISLAND
Foveaux Strait
STEWART ISLAND
SOUTHWEST CAPE
Invercargill
Dunedin
CAPE SAUNDERS
Timaru
Canterbury Bight
Christchurch
Pegasus Bay
TASMAN SEA
NEW ZEALAND
PACIFIC OCEAN
Same scale as main map

OTHER BOOKS BY THE EDITORS OF LIFE

LIFE WORLD LIBRARY

AUSTRALIA
AND
NEW ZEALAND

by Colin MacInnes

and The Editors of LIFE

A STONEHENGE BOOK

TIME INCORPORATED   NEW YORK

COVER: A mob of sheep, mustered
by two stockmen and a dog, streams
across a dusty range on a station, or ranch,
in South Australia. In such dry,
sparsely settled regions, stations
can be a million or more acres in area.

ABOUT THE WRITER

Colin MacInnes, author of the interpretive text for this volume in the LIFE World Library, is a British novelist and essayist who was brought up in Australia. Born in London in 1914, Mr. MacInnes was taken to Australia at the age of five by his mother, the popular novelist Angela Thirkell, and was educated in the schools of Hobart and Melbourne. Leaving for Europe at the age of 17, he worked for a business firm in Belgium, then moved to London and became a painter. During World War II, he first served in the infantry and later transferred to British intelligence units. After the war, he began to write for magazines, gaining a reputation as a perceptive, and often acerbic, social critic. His first novel, *To the Victors the Spoils*, was published in 1950 and has been followed by *June in Her Spring, City of Spades, Absolute Beginners* and *Mr. Love and Justice*. A collection of essays, *England, Half English*, was published in 1961. While preparing this volume, Mr. MacInnes spent several months traveling in Australia and New Zealand, becoming re-acquainted with the land where he grew up.

Contents

TIME-LIFE BOOKS

EDITOR
Norman P. Ross

TEXT DIRECTOR   ART DIRECTOR
William Jay Gold   Edward A. Hamilton

CHIEF OF RESEARCH
Beatrice T. Dobie

Assistant Text Director: Jerry Korn
Assistant Chief of Research: Monica O. Horne

•

PUBLISHER
Rhett Austell

General Manager: John A. Watters
Business Manager: John D. McSweeney
Circulation Manager: Joan D. Lanning

LIFE MAGAZINE

EDITOR: Edward K. Thompson
MANAGING EDITOR: George P. Hunt
PUBLISHER: Jerome S. Hardy

LIFE WORLD LIBRARY

Editorial Staff for *Australia and New Zealand:*
EDITOR: Oliver E. Allen
Assistant Editor: David S. Thomson
Designer: Ben Schultz
Chief Researcher: Grace Brynolson
Researchers: Jill Adams, Barbara Ballantine, Rebecca Chaitin,
Irene Ertugrul, Evelyn Hauptman, Madeleine Richards
Picture Researchers: Margaret K. Goldsmith, Joan T. Lynch
Art Associate: Robert L. Young
Art Assistants: James D. Smith, John M. Woods
Copy Staff: Marian Gordon Goldman, Patricia Miller, Dolores A. Littles

The interpretive text for the chapters of this book was written by
Colin MacInnes and the picture essays were written by Edmund
V. White. Many of the photographs were taken by David Moore.
Valuable help was provided by the following individuals and de-
partments of Time Inc.: Doris O'Neil, Chief of the LIFE Picture
Library; Content Peckham, Chief of the Bureau of Editorial Refer-
ence; and Richard M. Clurman, Chief of the TIME-LIFE News Service.

Introduction

Events since Pearl Harbor have brought about a marked change in the political horizons of Australia and New Zealand. The traumatic experiences of the fall of Singapore, the Battle of the Coral Sea and the bombing of Australia by Japanese planes have caused a reassessment of their problems of security. Moreover, the rumblings of restless, reinvigorated Asia have shifted the sights of both countries from the Middle East, where they had rested since World War I days, to the near north.

Geographically a part of Asia, Australia seemingly is becoming more and more aware of the southward pressures of that continent's millions, influenced and goaded by an aggressive Communist China. Slightly less vulnerable and more isolated across the Tasman Sea, New Zealand, too, is becoming conscious of new forces in the far Western Pacific area.

Australians and New Zealanders, however, are made of stern stuff. Today's prosperity and political stability tend to mask the toughening influences of their early histories. The beginnings of Australia, for example, were marked by violence, minor-scale rebellion and pitiless exploitation of man by man. Life was hard, and the harshness of climate and country exacted its toll. Fortunately for Australia, the great political and economic troubles in England and on the continent of Europe in the 1840s and 1850s coincided to some extent with the gold rush of the 1850s. These events brought about large-scale emigration to Australia of new classes of Englishmen, Irishmen, Scots and Welshmen, as well as Germans and others from the continent. Through their influence, the tightly knit establishment that had ruled Australia for decades was challenged, and new leadership came to the fore. Similar movements took place in New Zealand, where the discovery of gold in the early 1860s caused the population to double within five years.

Stemming largely from the fierce democracy in the gold fields and on the waterfronts of both countries, and led and inspired by this new brand of liberal leaders, trade unionism rose rapidly and through its militancy was largely responsible for many innovations in social security and labor legislation. In these fields Australia and, more particularly, New Zealand have led the world for more than half a century. They continue to do so today.

Australia and New Zealand play a highly important role in the attainment of the national objectives of the United States in the Pacific and Asian areas, as we do in theirs. Aside from the mutual obligations of the ANZUS and SEATO treaties, our rapidly growing trade with these countries and the interchange of more goods, investments, scientific knowledge and binational undertakings of various kinds all contribute to the healthy parallelism in foreign policy objectives between us.

This timely and much-needed volume prepared by Colin MacInnes and the Editors of LIFE is a penetrating and stimulating study. Mr. MacInnes has portrayed the Australians and New Zealanders for what they are: young, spirited, undaunted and unafraid of the challenges on every hand; people with a love of sunlight, movement and space. His analyses of their literature and art suggest a recurrent note of dissent, vigorous and impressive. And his comments and conclusions are forthright, sometimes challenging, but not to be taken lightly.

This book will do much to encourage American readers to pursue the fascinating and dramatic stories of those fine people, the Aussies and the Kiwis. I commend it to them.

WILLIAM J. SEBALD
former U.S. Ambassador to Australia

Sports-minded boys and girls from Sydney, Australia, tanned from swimming and surfing, line up at nearby Bondi Beach to watch a

8

major event in the annual Australian Surfboard Championships.

1

Two Distant, Strange and Rugged Lands

IF we look at a globe, we may see that there are three great land masses in the world which extend from the Northern to the Southern Hemispheres. First, the two Americas. Next, Europe connected via the Middle East to Africa. And then, the huge area of Asia, which breaks up at the equator into a chain of islands culminating in the largest of them all, Australia, and its companion state, New Zealand. Thus, though Australia and New Zealand are not Asian nations, they belong geographically to the Asian orbit.

And they are the only countries peopled predominantly by men of European origin which do so. The United States, powerful and densely populated, has Canada as a large neighbor of similar ethnic origins. The peoples of Europe, though their nations are small in size, are surrounded by rich and populous countries of the same history and stock. But Australians and New Zealanders are a mere 13.5 million English-speaking people with hundreds of millions of peoples to the near north of them whose societies are completely different from their own.

Two Distant, Strange and Rugged Lands

Australia (whose name derives from the Latin word *australis*, meaning "southern") may be large—it constitutes an entire continent in itself, almost as big as the United States not counting Alaska—and New Zealand may be 1,000 miles in length. Yet in this Asian world, these countries stand alone. To the west of them is the vastness of the Indian Ocean; to the east, the enormous extent of the Pacific; to the south, great empty seas until one reaches Antarctica; while to the north lies the world's greatest land mass, brimming over with peoples in whose social, political and religious customs Australia and New Zealand have no share whatever.

What other features distinguish these two countries from others of European stock? First, their extreme youth. The earliest settlers arrived in Australia at a time when Americans, already long established as a people, were winning their independence from the British. New Zealand was settled even later, a mere century and a half ago. The people of the United States may think theirs is a young country, but by comparison with that of Australia and New Zealand, America's history is already old.

In few other countries of the world is there such a sensation of *emptiness* as in Australia and New Zealand: not just in barren localities, but, save in the few big coastal cities, everywhere throughout these lands. Australia extends over nearly three million square miles and has thus, with its population of 11 million, less than four people to each square mile. New Zealand, with its much smaller area of more than 103,000 square miles and its population of 2.5 million, has about 24 people to the square mile—still a low figure by global standards.

In both countries, all the big cities are on the sea, and in Australia all six state capitals are, too, plus the capital of the Northern Territory (which, like Alaska before it achieved statehood, is federally administered). The only important exceptions in Australia are the federal capital, Canberra, which was created out of nothing for political reasons; several

NATIVE ANIMALS, the kangaroo and the emu, stand on acacia branches in the Australian coat of arms and support a shield decorated with emblems of the six states.

mining towns sited on their raw materials; and a number of agricultural townships. In New Zealand, the four largest cities of the two islands, including the national capital of Wellington, are also located on the coast. This sea-fringe culture resembles that of certain Latin American republics whose cities also cling close to the shore, and there is nothing whatever of the vast concentrations of population in large inland towns that are to be found in Europe and the United States.

Why is this? First, of course, it is because the populations are so small. Even in America, the earliest settlements were coastal, and it was not until population and prosperity both grew that Americans pushed inland to build great cities far from the sea. Next, there are the barriers of nature. In Australia, a narrow "fertile crescent" of mountains, rivers and good rainfall stretches from the extreme north down along the east coast to the southeastern part of the country; beyond this the great mass of the continent is largely barren or even outright desert. In New Zealand, huge mountain ranges run up the spines of both the North and the South Islands, confining habitation to the coastal zones. Thus, in both countries, but particularly in Australia, the people turn their backs on the interior. Of course, if Australia's population were larger, a "colonization" of its inner regions would no doubt be undertaken, despite the great natural obstacles. But at present the movement inland is tentative, and one almost has the impression, when one sees the big coastal towns and then the huge empty hinterlands, that the Australians, so recently arrived from overseas to claim this country for their own, still do so with uncertainty, and cling to the "safe" seas from whence they came.

In all evolved nations today, the tendency is for an imbalance between urban and rural populations, for industry demands huge city concentrations, and thanks to agricultural mechanization fewer and fewer countrymen are needed to sustain the industrial workers of the cities. However, in Australia and in

New Zealand, this imbalance of town and country assumes almost fantastic proportions. Thus, in Australia more than *half* the total population lives in the six state capitals. In New Zealand—despite its economy being still principally agricultural—two fifths of the people live in the four largest cities. Any vision one may have of two predominantly rural countries, consisting chiefly of huge sheep and cattle "stations" and of dairy farms, must thus be substantially corrected. The stations and farms are there, all right; but so is Sydney, with its more than two million people, and so is Auckland, New Zealand, with one fifth of its nation's population.

Let us now examine each country separately to see in what ways each may be said, without exaggeration, to be unique. Australia, in the first place, is the only continent on the globe that is inhabited by a single nation— and almost wholly by a single race. True, Australia may be the smallest continent. But there is none of the immense racial and political diversity that is found in all of its larger fellows.

Australia is the only big nation that was founded without internal war or revolution. The histories of Europe and of Asia

THE TWO PEOPLES of New Zealand are represented on its coat of arms by a white woman and a Maori warrior. The crown symbolizes allegiance to Britain's monarch.

are made up almost entirely of civil and foreign wars. Even America, though founded so much later, has vivid memories of battles fought on American soil. Now certainly, Australian soldiers have won high honor in battles overseas. But at home, except for minor skirmishes, peace has reigned from the beginning. One of the few significant dates in Australian history is that of its founding in 1788.

But though so young historically, Australia in geologic terms is an ancient land, perhaps one of the most ancient. The "alpine storm" that threw up the mighty mountain ranges of all the other continents passed Australia by. The tallest mountain on the continent, Kosciusko, is a mere 7,316 feet high, and all such features making for scenic variety are concentrated in the southeast, close to the sea. In the vast inland tracts which, in terms of area, may

be said to be the "real" Australia, there is a huge monotony of semiarid scrub and desert, broken only by ranges of eroded cliffs and the huge eccentric monoliths of the "red center."

Peculiar to the country, too, are its highly distinctive flora and fauna. The two chief trees are the gum, or eucalyptus, and the wattle, or acacia. The acacia is akin to the mimosa of the United States, and bursts into honeyed brilliance in the spring. More characteristic, however, is the eucalyptus, whose 600 varieties range from majestic mountain species soaring 300 feet to stunted shrubs whose long roots, probing for subterranean water in the arid areas, enable them to survive years of drought.

About the eucalyptus, which, like the maple tree of Canada, is a symbol of the country, there is something invincibly Australian; and if it be true, as it must be, that humans are influenced by their environment, there may seem to be, in the appearance of the gum tree, characteristics that reflect those of the Australian temperament itself. For this tree is casual, graceless, eccentric, robust and everlasting. It scatters its bark untidily on the parched soil, bends itself into awkward but vigorous shapes, and drops its thin gray leaves messily in times of drought. It seems an indifferent, sardonic tree, denying formal beauty. In their cities, Australians seem ashamed of the evergreen (or green-gray) eucalyptus and replace it by decorous deciduous trees imported from overseas. But out in the vast "bush," the eucalyptus reigns supreme, filling the hot air with its sour, pungent odor and giving to the aloof, monotonous landscape a raw, wild, unwelcoming poetry of its own.

The fauna is highly peculiar and, even to those who do not know Australia, justly renowned. The near-monopoly of marsupials (animals that carry their young in a pouch), of which only the opossum of America is to be found outside Australia, is believed to be due to the isolation of the continent in prehistoric eras. Chief of these is the kangaroo, which, with the ostrichlike emu, forms Australia's

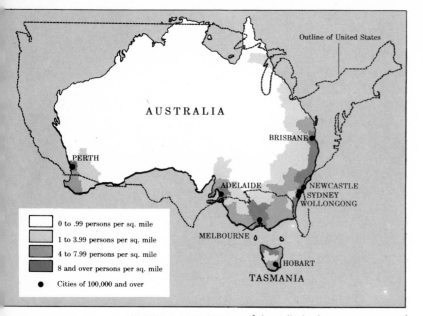

SPARSE POPULATION of Australia is shown on a map of population density and distribution. Some small cities exist in the seemingly unpopulated areas, but they are not large enough to raise the average. For comparison, an outline of the United States at the same scale is shown. The population of the continental U.S. as shown is 185.1 million; Australia's is 11 million.

Map legend:

- 0 to .99 persons per sq. mile
- 1 to 3.99 persons per sq. mile
- 4 to 7.99 persons per sq. mile
- 8 and over persons per sq. mile
- ● Cities of 100,000 and over

coat of arms. To meet face to face, the kangaroo is not such an amiable animal as the sight of it leaping balletically in the distance might suggest, for it is decidedly squirrel-like in appearance, and if it does not care for you, its huge hind legs can pack a wicked punch. Much beloved of visitors is the koala bear—tourists feel they must be photographed holding one—which lives exclusively on eucalyptus leaves, does not normally drink water and, despite its cuddly mien, can scratch your eyes out with a set of serviceable saber claws if it is handled improperly. The birth of its offspring—that miraculous moment when the newborn fetus, barely an inch long, scrambles upward to its mother's pouch to suckle there—has rarely been observed since it occurs so seldom. Later on the infant koala sits engagingly on its mother's back, like the child of an Indian squaw.

Most bizarre of all Australia's creatures is the duck-billed platypus, which stands between the modern mammal and the creatures of prehistory. It has a ducklike bill, webbed feet and a fur coat, and is amphibious. It hatches its young from eggs, then suckles them. This strange, timid creature is difficult to see, and it is heavily protected—as are the rare marsupials—by the Government. Another interesting nonmarsupial is the dingo, a yellow hound

which came to Australia long ago from Asia. It can sometimes be tamed but, like the kangaroo, is more usually shot, because the kangaroo takes grass needed for sheep and cattle, and the dingo, alone or in pairs, attacks them.

The most celebrated Australian birds are the lyrebird, a prodigious mimic, whose love dance, in which the male agitates his extravagant, arched tail feathers to attract his female admirers, has inspired the Australian choreographer Robert Helpmann to create his recent ballet, *The Display;* the red-beaked black swan, which Australia has produced to show the world it can be different; and the kookaburra, or "laughing jackass," appropriately named since its raucous, insulting cackle mocks the intruder. Among a profusion of reptiles, there is the goanna, a six-foot-long "dragon" of repellent aspect who, if it suddenly meets a horse—or a human being—is likely to mistake it for a tree and try to claw its way up for safety, with embarrassing results.

But most particular of all to Australia is that in this continent alone (except, perhaps, for some remoter parts of Africa and South America), there exists a still-surviving prehistoric people—the Australian aborigines. More than 40,000 of them remain in the continent and, though most are now detribalized, thousands still live in conditions of a Stone Age culture, much as our own ancestors must have done tens of thousands of years ago. In this primitive existence they are a dying race, and frantic efforts are being made by Australian anthropologists to record what amounts to a living museum of history before it is too late.

And now let us consider how New Zealand, in its very different ways, may be said also to be unique. The first factor we may notice is that this country is surely the most isolated civilized nation on the globe. Australia may seem remote enough; but New Zealand is 1,200 miles farther off to the southeast and, except for the southern tip of Chile, is the last sizable human bastion between the inhabited earth and the ice packs of the Antarctic. And one cannot visit New Zealand without becoming aware of the effects of this remoteness on the national economy and temperament.

The visitor will next notice how, by comparison with the monotony of much of Australia, New

Zealand is infinitely varied. New Zealanders boast, not without justification, that every kind of scenery may be found in their two islands. On the South Island, there are the great mountains, streams, fiords and lakes that may remind the visitor of Norway. On the North Island, there is scenery that may in turn recall, as the traveler progresses, the grandeur of the Pyrenees, the aridity of Arabia, the elegance of Italy and, when the extreme north is reached, the rich verdure of the tropics.

The next peculiarity is that New Zealand, with a Maori population of 180,000, or 7 per cent of the total, can almost be called the chief Polynesian country of the world. Although the vast majority of New Zealanders are Europeans, there are more Polynesians in this country than on any other island of the Pacific. They are a people entirely distinct, racially, from the Australian aborigines, and, again unlike the aborigines, they occupy an important place in their country's national life.

ONCE again we find indigenous fauna, which bears no relation to Australia's—though certain Australian animals have been imported. The first curiosity is that there are no native mammals except for two species of bat; a dog and a rat were introduced by the Maoris, the latter unintentionally. But it is the flightless birds that are the most characteristic, chief of which is the kiwi, a nocturnal beast which most New Zealanders have never seen (except in a zoo), even though they call themselves "Kiwis"—a nomenclature which we, too, may now adopt, since "New Zealander" is something of a mouthful. A recent discovery was that of the big takahe, a bird long thought to be extinct, and this has caused some optimists to speculate that the country's most fabulous bird, the moa, may still survive. The moa, flightless like the kiwi, was a giant of up to 10 feet in height, and many skeletal remains of it have been found. We may conclude by noticing that New Zealand has no snakes, like Ireland, but unlike Australia, which has dozens of horrible varieties. Also that the tuatara, a lizardlike reptile surviving from prehistoric times, is New Zealand's rival to Australia's goanna in ugliness.

But what is most strange about New Zealand remains to be said. For until the Maoris arrived, well into the Christian era, there were *no* permanent settlers in New Zealand. For tens of thousands of years elsewhere, humanity had battled from its earliest origins to build great cultures which, with the centuries, have in turn been replaced by others. But during all these ages and throughout all this human drama, in New Zealand there was nothing.

To speak once again of both countries, we may now see how the cultures of both Australia and New Zealand are by necessity peripheral. That is to say, though these nations belong politically and economically to the Western world, they are cut off by recent history and by eternal geography from the two great centers of Western civilization, Europe and the United States. There is thus, in the Australian and New Zealand soul, a perpetual division. On the one hand, the inhabitants of these two countries have a profound desire to create their own social orders and cultural lives. But on the other hand, there is the magnetic cultural and economic pull of Europe and America, with their older histories, deeper cultural development and greater riches. In addition, since the resurgence of Asian nations in the past two decades, Australia and New Zealand must come to terms with their huge, clamant neighbors to the north. How both peoples have tried to resolve this conflict of interest and ideal, we shall shortly try to examine.

TWO words to the reader, though, before we begin. Although Australia and New Zealand do form politically and sociologically a more or less coherent group, the reader will have already grasped that they do differ considerably, especially in terms of geography and economics. There is perhaps a parallel, on a much larger scale, between America and Canada. The two nations may have much in common but also a great deal that is distinctive.

The next is a reminder that we are in the Southern Hemisphere, so that the reader must think of going *north* to heat and the equator and *south* to cold and the Antarctic. He must also remember that the seasons are reversed here: North America's summer is Australia's and New Zealand's winter; and in December, when the United States and northern Europe are freezing, Australians and Kiwis are enjoying a hot Christmas dinner in a heat wave.

Girls in elegantly correct riding habits parade slowly past the spectators in the opening event of an agricultural show in Oxford, a New

A Blend of Old Ways and New Exuberance

The way of life in Australia and New Zealand is a unique blend of an American kind of informality with a British heritage of polite institutions. This duality expresses itself in a universal zest for athletics and the outdoors, which a thriving economy, an ideal

LAWN BOWLING occupies members of the Leichhardt Bowling Club in Mount Isa, a mining town in Queensland, Australia. The club is equipped with a swimming pool and tennis courts.

BILLIARD GAME engrosses two fishermen *(below)* at a hotel bar in Lancelin on Western Australia's coast. The region is well known for its abundant crayfish, or "rock lobsters."

Zealand farm town on the South Island's Canterbury Plains.

climate and vast expanses of open territory promote. Australians and New Zealanders are particularly fond of English sports—but engage in them with the enthusiastic, rough-and-ready spirit which characterized the United States at the turn of the last century.

CHEERING SECTION of Maori girls in school uniforms *(left)* encourages fellow team members during a basketball game in Kawerau, New Zealand. The Maoris, the original Polynesian settlers of New Zealand, are fully integrated with the whites, whom they call *pakehas*. Most schools, even those which emphasize Maori culture, admit both Maori and *pakeha* students.

SPIRITED DETERMINATION marks the faces of the players during a Rugby match *(below)* in Palmerston North between two New Zealand university teams, Massey and Auckland. In Rugby Union, the game that is being played here, each team has 15 members. New Zealand, which competes with France, South Africa, Britain and Australia, is often world champion.

SMALL-TOWN RODEO in Donnybrook, Western Australia, rings with cheers as a young cowgirl does her best to stay astride a bucking calf. Australia's rodeos are carefully patterned after their older American counterparts, but Donnybrook's is only one event in the area's annual Apple Festival, a sort of country fair which includes sings, dancing, parades and treasure hunts.

YOUNG SAILORS who belong to the Vaucluse Sailing Club in Sydney, Australia, rig and launch their sabot-class dinghies for competition. Races often take place in Sydney Harbor's open waters, although a sudden squall can capsize an entire fleet.

ATTENTIVE BOYS watch for underwater life *(right)* in the river Avon, which runs through Christchurch on the South Island of New Zealand. Since the seasons are reversed below the equator, a cool autumn day like this one occurs in April.

CASUAL FISHERMEN cast their lines *(opposite)* near Christchurch, New Zealand, where the Avon and Heathcote Rivers converge to flow into the ocean. In some regions, fish are so numerous that the Government allows fishing the year round.

A FIRE BRIGADE displays close teamwork during a demonstration by Western Australian volunteer firemen at Fremantle. Presented as a sports contest every year, these displays of modern fire-fighting techniques by various teams were first organized in 1899. The 51 brigades in the state have 1,200 members.

THERMAL POOLS near Whakarewarewa in New Zealand are used by Maori boys for cooking chestnuts. For centuries the Maoris have done their cooking by putting food into baskets and lowering them into the steam fissures and boiling water. Now a tourist attraction, the pools allegedly can cure sickness.

In a drawing of Sydney made in 1792, just four years after a British penal colony had been established there, a band of aborigines

(foreground) surveys the ships lying at anchor in the city's harbor.

2

Captain Cook's Children

THE history of Australia begins properly with the arrival of the aborigines, around 25,000 B.C., just as New Zealand's does with that of the Maoris, around 1350 A.D. But since we shall meet more fully with both of these peoples in Chapter 7, we may start our story of Australia and New Zealand with the coming of the first Europeans.

To begin with Australia, the great surprise is that it was discovered so late in history. The great Asian and Polynesian navigators had discovered the Pacific islands, but if they had ever sailed south to Australia, they must have found it a forbidding place and sheared off in dismay toward more fertile lands.

The Portuguese and the Spaniards investigated the area in the 16th Century but did not land on Australia. The first European explorers actually to set foot on the continent were the Dutch, in the early 17th Century, and the earliest navigator really to examine it was Abel Tasman, who, in 1642, discovered the island now called Tasmania and the west coast of New Zealand, and then charted the inhospitable north Australian shores. The first Englishman to sight the continent was William Dampier, an ex-pirate, who saw only the northwest regions.

The Columbus of Australia and New Zealand is really Captain James Cook, who, in 1768, was sent by the British Government to Tahiti under orders to observe from there the transit of Venus, and who was then instructed to find, if he could, the legendary "Southland" about which Europeans were increasingly curious. Since he approached from the east, following a generally southern route which kept him away from the formidable Great Barrier Reef, Cook had the great advantage of seeing both the beauty of New Zealand and the southeastern coasts of the Australian continent. He circumnavigated New Zealand, explored the unknown east coast of Australia, and in 1770 sailed into Botany Bay. After taking possession of the country in the name of King George III, he called it New South Wales.

IN 1779, Sir Joseph Banks, the botanist who had accompanied Cook and, with him, named Botany, suggested to the British House of Commons that the Bay would be an excellent place on which to dump English convicts sentenced to transportation. Hitherto these unfortunates had been dispatched to the Americas, but the revolt of the colonists there had now made this impossible, and newly discovered Australia seemed an excellent alternative.

Accordingly, in 1787, some 750 convicts, of whom a quarter were women and a third of these professional harlots, embarked from Portsmouth under the care of Arthur Phillip, first governor of Australia. Sailing west via South America, the convoy landed at Botany Bay in January 1788. But finding the country around it arid and waterless, the governor set off to the north in a small boat and sailed through what is now Sydney Heads to discover what he called "the finest harbour in the world." Though greeted with howls by the aborigines, the convoy anchored at Sydney Cove, and Australia's history began.

Australians are understandably sensitive about their convict origins; yet it must be recorded that, before transportation was finally abolished in 1868, some 168,000 convicts were sent out to Australia. Apologists have sometimes suggested that these were mere innocents sentenced for stealing a sheep or robbing an apple orchard, but research has proved that many

of them were hardened criminals who had narrowly escaped hanging. Of course, conditions of life among the poorer classes in 18th and 19th Century England were such that it was easy to become a criminal. And, of course, a criminal tendency is by no means necessarily transmitted to a criminal's offspring. And again, the number of free settlers who came later greatly exceeded the criminal immigration. Nevertheless, the fact remains that many of Australia's founding fathers were delinquents, and this may well account for certain features of the Australian temperament: for the violence, the sense of comradeship in adversity, the predominantly male character of the society and the generally skeptical attitude toward authority.

From the beginning, class divisions on the English pattern were enforced upon the infant colony. Land filched from the aborigines was granted to officers, and the convicts, after completing their prison labors, could work for this new upper class in exchange for payment in rum. Among these early settlers the most prominent was John Macarthur, who, at the turn of the century, first introduced Merino sheep on a large scale to the continent, and thus laid the foundation of Australia's subsequent prosperity. Among early governors, the worst was William Bligh, of *Bounty* fame, who was deposed at the prompting of Macarthur; the best was Lachlan Macquarie, the "father of Australia," who embarked on a massive policy of public works, among them a new hospital which he succeeded in getting built without public funds by the ingenious stratagem of awarding the contractors a three-year monopoly on the import of rum and other spirits to the colony.

NEXT came the internal explorers of Australia, unknown outside their continent, but national heroes in its folklore. George Bass and Matthew Flinders explored Van Diemen's Land—the island, later to be named Tasmania, which is separated from Australia by what is now called Bass Strait—and Flinders circumnavigated the continent. In 1813 William Charles Wentworth, William Lawson and Gregory Blaxland penetrated the Blue Mountains west of Sydney and discovered the pastoral country that lay beyond. Charles Sturt found the rich river basins between what are now Victoria and New South Wales. In 1840-1841 Edward John Eyre traversed

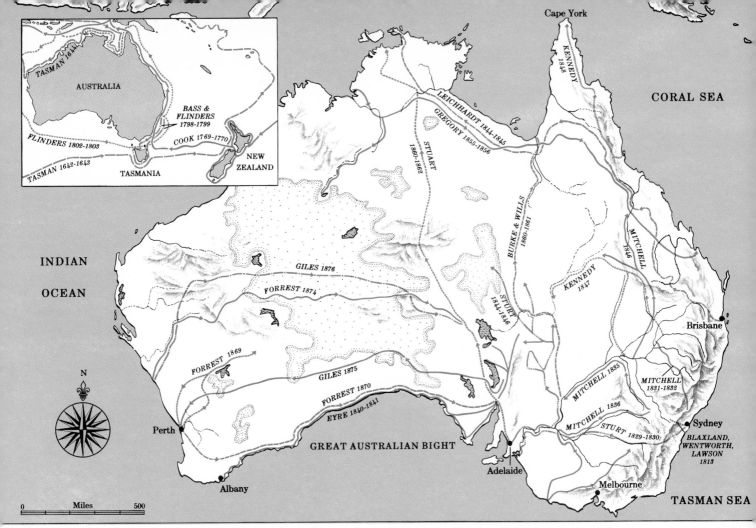

INDIAN OCEAN

CORAL SEA

Cape York

GREAT AUSTRALIAN BIGHT

TASMAN SEA

N

Miles
0   500

Perth

Albany

Adelaide

Melbourne

Sydney

Brisbane

Inset map:

AUSTRALIA

TASMAN 1642

FLINDERS 1802-1803

TASMAN 1642-1643

TASMANIA

BASS & FLINDERS 1798-1799

COOK 1769-1770

NEW ZEALAND

Large map labels:

KENNEDY 1848

LEICHHARDT 1844-1845

GREGORY 1855-1856

STUART 1860-1862

BURKE & WILLS 1860-1861

MITCHELL 1846

KENNEDY 1847

STURT 1844-1846

GILES 1876

FORREST 1874

FORREST 1869

GILES 1875

FORREST 1870

EYRE 1840-1841

MITCHELL 1835

MITCHELL 1836

MITCHELL 1831-1832

STURT 1829-1830

BLAXLAND, WENTWORTH, LAWSON 1813

ROUTES OF DISCOVERY AND EXPLORATION followed by the men who opened up Australia and New Zealand are shown above. Both countries were first investigated extensively by Abel Tasman, but European settlement began only after the voyages of Cook *(inset map)*. Many of those who explored the interior of Australia *(large map)* suffered severely. Ludwig Leichhardt, after journeying to the northern tip, tried to traverse the continent from east to west; heat and drought forced him back and on his second attempt he was lost. Edmund Kennedy was killed by aborigines on the Cape York Peninsula. Burke and Wills died of starvation returning from an expedition to the north coast. Many other explorers perished from exhaustion or disappeared.

the enormous distance from South Australia to the distant west. And then—to leap ahead a bit—in 1861 Robert O'Hara Burke met his death in the huge central spaces of Australia.

Meanwhile, in the wake of these discoveries, the infant colony slowly expanded. To forestall the possibility of French occupation, a party was sent south from Sydney in 1803 to Port Phillip Bay, in what is now Australia's second most populous state, Victoria, and a small settlement was founded on Van Diemen's Land. Later, Van Diemen's Land achieved a notoriety when the most recalcitrant convicts of New South Wales were dispatched to a greater hell at Port Arthur, in the south of the island. Today, Port Arthur's ruined barracks, jails and church,

surrounded by laundered sward, may seem "romantic." But then one remembers that starved mastiffs were chained close together across Eaglehawk Neck, and that escaping convicts had the choice of dodging the ravenous hounds or the profusion of sharks on either side of the spit if they braved the seas.

By 1819 there were 26,000 souls in New South Wales and 4,000 in Van Diemen's Land, rather less than half of them convicts. For by this time free immigrants were arriving, who, with the sons of convicts, were the first large group of Australians not by necessity but by choice. Among them were a number of Irish Roman Catholics, thanks to the repressive measures of the English in their native Ireland, although the governmental "establishment"

25

in New South Wales was rigorously Protestant. This was to be an important factor in early Australian social and political life, wherein the Roman Catholics represented the radical, protesting element. By now the underlying Australian social pattern consisted on the one hand of the poor free settlers and the "emancipists"—freed convicts—and on the other of the "pastoralists"—landowners largely of English origin who were accorded land, wealth and privilege by the Government.

In 1823 a semblance of home rule appeared when a legislative council was created to advise the governor, but this failed to satisfy the emancipists, who were now led by William Charles Wentworth, the affluent explorer who earlier had traversed the Blue Mountains. By 1825 Van Diemen's Land was a separate colony, and in 1829 a colony was founded on the Swan River, subsequently to grow into what is today Western Australia. In 1834 a new colony called South Australia was established. The youngest colony of all, Queensland, was founded in 1859.

BEGINNING in the 1830s, free immigrants started to come in larger numbers. In the next two decades more than 200,000 Britons immigrated, and a "bounty" system for immigrants—such as still exists today—was introduced to attract promising settlers to the region. Some of these men were poor artisans, but many were "gentlemen" farmers and, indeed, needy adventurers who came to form what was known as the "squattocracy"—men who simply "squatted" on vast tracts of land, with or without the approval of the Government. The pretensions of this "landed gentry," who sought to implant in the young continent the social traditions of distant England, aroused the ire of the egalitarian emancipists.

The squatters, who after 1841 were barred from using free convict labor, wanted to import coolies from Asia, and this did occur to some extent. But the emancipist proletarians violently opposed such importation of cheap labor, and it was thus that the still-continuing "White Australia Policy" first began: not as a matter of official decision so much as a protest by the underprivileged against the threat they saw to their own living standards.

By means of an act passed in 1842, the Legislative Council of New South Wales became partly elective, and the political scene there was dominated by three groups: the Government, or "establishment," party; the landowners, represented by Macarthur and Wentworth; and the city radicals—the merchants and poorer classes. In these groups, there may perhaps be seen the beginnings of the Liberal, Country and Labour Parties of today.

FROM the outset the "states' rights" movement was even stronger than that in the United States, and though actual conflict was avoided, federation did not come to Australia until as recently as 1901. Customs duties were levied at each colonial border, and there was the absurdity, after railroads came in 1854, of no less than three different railway gauges in the different colonies.

In 1851 came an event which, more than any other since the arrival of the first convicts, transformed Australia. In that year E. H. Hargraves, returning from the gold fields of California, discovered gold in New South Wales; soon a big strike was made in Victoria, in the town of Ballarat. The gold rush was on, and from all over Australia—and soon from all the world—diggers poured into the gold fields. The importance of this was not so much in the wealth the young colonies acquired as in the political and social consequences. Labor deserted the towns and the big sheep and cattle stations, and thus became even more costly. A new proletariat of rootless egalitarians came into existence. Their political temper was radical, and demands were now raised for the abolition of the license fee for gold digging, for lower land prices and for political equality. The commotion included what has been called "the only battle fought on Australian soil"—the episode of the Eureka Stockade. In 1854 several hundred gold diggers erected a stockade in the Eureka Lead mining area in Ballarat, from which a number of them temporarily defied the military. Racial trouble followed when Chinese diggers—ancestors of the present Chinese minority in Australia—were attacked in the Buckland River riots.

Despite their defeat, the resistance of the Eureka diggers, combined with the gold rush itself, did result in material progress and an expansion of democracy. Universal male suffrage was presently made law in two colonies, and by the 1880s, education was becoming free, compulsory and secular. Legislation was introduced whereby "selectors" could occupy small "selections" on newly opened land, the development of which had hitherto been monopolized by the pastoralist "squattocracy." By 1861 the population of the colonies had grown to 1.2 million, and a decade later a majority of the population was native-born. Perhaps almost as vital as the gold rush was the innovation of refrigerated ships. In 1880 the *Strathleven*—the first of many such vessels—carried its cargo of frozen meat successfully from Sydney to Great Britain, and this enabled Australia to become a great exporting nation.

BY the turn of the century, there was a growing demand for federation. This was impelled by the feeling that external defense and economic advance could never be achieved by the colonies alone. A series of bank disasters and strikes made the colonial structure seem even more inadequate; meanwhile, there was increasing clamor, voiced by the rising Labour Party, for welfare legislation in the form of factory acts, abolition of plural voting, industrial arbitration, old-age pensions and minimum wages. After intercolonial conferences and a referendum, federation finally arrived in 1901, the six colonies becoming states in the new Commonwealth. Australians never do anything by halves, and in time the federal powers exceeded those of the states to a degree even greater than that in the United States.

With federation, modern Australian history begins. Little more than a decade later, the nation was reborn, in a profound sense, in the World War I battles for Gallipoli. Postwar politics were dominated by the Labour Party and the Nationalists, or conservatives, who, in a new grouping called the United Australian Party, were in office when World War II began. Most of the second war, however, was fought under the Labour Governments of John Curtin and then Joseph Chifley. A key declaration of Curtin's, at the time of the Japanese invasions throughout Asia, was that "without inhibition of any kind, I make it quite clear that Australia looks to America, free of any pangs as to our traditional links or kinship with the United Kingdom." The umbilical cord that had linked Australia to England was now finally and forever severed, and Australia emerged from the tutelage of a century and a half as a sovereign nation standing ultimately on its own.

Brief as Australia's history is, that of New Zealand is, if anything, even shorter. The country was named Staten Landt by Abel Tasman when he discovered it in 1642, but a year later the Dutch renamed it *Nieuw Zeeland*. The original settlers were not, as in Australia, convicts; nevertheless, according to the present-day New Zealand wit and scholar E. H. McCormick, while consisting of "evangelical zealots and pious artisans," they also included "shore-whalers and grog-shop keepers . . . dealers in flax and dried heads, escaped and time-expired convicts . . . sawyers and procurers and adventurers." But religious missions began early, and the conversion of the Maoris was soon undertaken. In 1840 Britain formally annexed New Zealand; for a year it was administered from New South Wales, but in 1841 it became a separate colony.

SERIOUS settlement now began, much prompted by the resourceful English publicist Edward Gibbon Wakefield. It was Wakefield's theory that if the discontented elements in England were transplanted to New Zealand, English society would no longer be threatened by the new egalitarian spirit, and a community based on the old social order could be born in the young colony. Founding the New Zealand Company to assist emigration, Wakefield prodded the British Government to help sustain the infant colony. Settlement soon extended in the North around the Bay of Islands and spread south.

Another task of the colonists was to come to terms with the Maori people, in whose country they had settled. In February 1840, there was signed the Treaty of Waitangi, by which the Maoris ceded sovereign rights to the British Crown. However, the Maoris did not cede their land, and many chiefs refused to sign the treaty, while others were not invited to do so. Despite the treaty, more and more of the lands were soon occupied, and the seeds of the later Maori Wars were swiftly sown.

By the late 1850s, hostility between Maori and *pakeha* (or European) was already coming to a head. The Europeans, though still partly dependent on the Maoris even for their food, were increasingly filching their precious land. Trade the Maoris could accept, and indeed welcomed, but not the loss of soil that was both held to be sacred and, since owned by tribes and individuals jointly, regarded not as private property but as a communal possession. In 1858 the Maoris, hitherto led by tribal chieftains, ominously elected a king to prevent the further deterioration of their rights.

The hostilities began in 1860, when the British unjustly purchased some land in Waitara; when the Maoris objected, the Europeans captured a tribal *pa*, or fortress. The ensuing conflict, which the Maoris called "the fire in the fern" or "the white man's anger," lasted intermittently for 12 years, and almost resulted in a Maori victory. Among the fiercest Maori warriors were the *hauhaus*, members of the fanatical religious movement called Pai Marire. When the Maoris were finally defeated, millions of acres of their land were impounded, and they withdrew into a sullen hostility. And it was several decades before these people, thanks to good health, social legislation and nationalist fervor, were able to regain some of their former power.

From the outset—and despite the aristocratic fantasies of Wakefield—New Zealand society was, as it has remained, essentially democratic. True, there were large sheep stations as in Australia, but there was no dominant ruling caste, and there was also a large number of smaller farmers. Workers would soon begin forming "combinations," or trade unions. A gold rush to Otago, on the South Island, reinforced the proletarian element.

THE modern expansion and development of New Zealand were begun under Sir Julius Vogel, a Londoner of great resource, energy and vulgarity. Arriving in 1861, he became treasurer and later prime minister of the infant state, and in 1876 abolished the provincial governments, so that New Zealand was never troubled, as Australia was, by a conflict of federal and state interests. Immigration proceeded apace, and Germans and Scandinavians arrived as well as British. In the 1870s, by crossing the Merino sheep with the Lincoln and other strains, there was bred the celebrated New Zealand Corriedale, a sheep yielding both wool and excellent meat. The dairy farming industry, now so vital to the country, was developed with grants of land to small "cow

cockie" farmers (so called because they descended on the soil like cockatoos), and these farms spread mostly on the warm and fertile North Island. In 1882 the *Dunedin* carried the first cargo of frozen meat to Britain, and New Zealand's destiny as a chief larder of the world began. A self-governing colony after 1852, New Zealand achieved Dominion status within the British Empire in 1907.

Under Sir George Grey, legislation made New Zealand in the late 19th Century the most socially evolved country in the world. "New Zealand is the birth place of the Twentieth Century," wrote the noted political scientist Frank Parsons in 1904, and laws laying the foundations of what would now be called a "welfare state" were already enacted by the turn of the century. The chief later sponsor of this social radicalism was Richard John Seddon, known somewhat undemocratically as "King Dick," under whom all aspects of rural and industrial life were regulated to the workingman's advantage. Even female suffrage came to New Zealand as early as 1893.

IN World War I the New Zealanders, though small in absolute numbers, were outstanding for their valor. The period between the wars saw the rise to power of the Labour Party, which ruled from 1935 to 1949, and which consolidated the social gains of earlier decades. But though New Zealand has known more Labour power than any other Anglo-Saxon country, this state socialism was chiefly effected not by nationalization but by Government control of marketing and credit. New Zealand is still, basically, a capitalist country; but with its almost total reliance on agricultural exports, and with one of the highest levels of trade per capita in the world, all parties are agreed that the high living standard can be maintained only by governmental control of the economy.

In World War II no Allied country other than Russia conscripted a greater percentage of its manpower than New Zealand, while in the subsequent era of peace the real per capita income exceeded that of any country in the world except the United States.

New Zealand is thus a country of great material achievement and of wide intervention of the state in social affairs, yet with an absolute determination, despite its isolation and limited resources, to make its mark in the world.

Grass trees, with their bushy clumps of leaves surmounted by tall spikes resembling cattails, decorate a hillside in New South Wales.

Unbroken Silences of a Remote, Varied World

Although much of Australia and New Zealand is now built up, a good part of the land has the same lonely grandeur it had before the white settlers arrived. More than a third of Australia, for example, is desert—expanses of barren sand only rarely broken by stark, jutting mountain ranges. The tropical swamplands along the Australian north coast and the highlands of Tasmania are wild and untouched. New Zealand's topography is more compressed—a glacier can flow into a region of orchids and ferns.

GAUNT SHAPES of the Mount Olga range *(opposite)* jut eerily out of the parched heartland of Australia's Northern Territory. Geologically ancient, they have been eroded by wind and rain.

MAMMOTH FORMATION, Ayers Rock *(right)* glows in the evening sun. A solid monolith of red sandstone in the "red center," the central desert area of Australia, the rock rises 1,143 feet.

GROTESQUE EROSION, which Australians call "The Brain" *(below)* because of its resemblance to a human skull, marks the north face of Ayers Rock, which here is inspected by a light airplane.

SPECTACULAR FIORD, Milford Sound on the southwestern coast of New Zealand's South Island has waters a mile deep which reflect the surrounding mountains. The 10-mile-long sound is one of many such fiords notched out of the coastline by glaciers thousands of years ago. One of the tallest mountains in the area is the 5,560-foot Mitre Peak *(center)*, which is heavily

forested at its base, since rainfall there often exceeds 200 inches a year. Once nearly inaccessible, the sound is now easily reached by light airplanes, boats and automobiles; a hotel at its head accommodates the growing numbers of tourists. Sightseers can hike along the trails which wind through neighboring mountains and the nearly 3.3 million acres of Fiordland National Park.

ICY DELTA on New Zealand's South Island joins the Dart River, which is fed by glaciers in the Southern Alps, to 52-mile-long Lake Wakatipu *(foreground)*. The lake, a holiday center, has long fascinated and puzzled scientists because its level inexplicably rises and falls three inches every five minutes.

FROZEN PLATEAU, the Big Mac snowfield in the Southern Alps of New Zealand *(right)* offers a clear landing place for two Cessnas bringing tourists to see nearby Fox Glacier. Flowing west toward the coast, the glacier drops 1,000 feet along every mile of its course until it ends only 670 feet above sea level.

3

A Vast, Half-empty Continent

WHERE is the "real" Australia? Is it in the bubbling big cities and the fertile pastures of the southeast? Or is it to be found in the huge, lonely cattle stations of the outback and the even remoter deserts of the "back-of-beyond"? Australians, justly proud of their big towns and thriving industries, may feel that to praise the raw solitudes of the interior is to be unrealistic and sentimental. Yet because in all Australian hearts there lingers a nostalgia for the bush life of the outback, a description of the country can perhaps best begin at the "red center" of the continent in the Northern Territory.

The territory, with 523,620 square miles, covers one sixth of the country but has only 50,000 people, of whom about one third are aborigines. For this

reason it has not yet become a state. Its chief cities —if one can call them such—are Darwin, the northern port and international air terminal with a population of 12,500, whose inhabitants call themselves "Top Enders," and Alice Springs, whose 5,000 people make it the largest township of central Australia.

"The Alice" (the names of many outback townships are prefaced by a "The" in popular speech) is so called in memory of Lady Alice Todd, the wife of the engineer who pioneered the overland telegraph line in the days when camel trains were the main link with the outside world. In that era, there were no "springs" at The Alice, for the Todd River, whose bed cuts through the city, still fills up only in the rare wet seasons. But artesian water has been found, often only four feet underground, and this explains the extent and fertile look of the town. It has a delightful winter climate, rarely falling below 70° F. during the day, although in the summer it is hot. What most lures tourists to The Alice, however, is the existence, some 275 miles to the southwest, of the most remarkable natural features in all Australia, the Mount Olga formation and Ayers Rock.

EMBARKING in a local aircraft, the visitor will first soar over the red-ochered Macdonnell Ranges, huge eroded mountains twisted through the centuries into fantastic lunar shapes, as if some giant cook had stirred the big rocks into a hideous pudding. Then the land flattens, and though parched and hostile on the ground, the vast plains seem from this height to have an exquisite, tender beauty, with soft hues of rose, pale emerald green and misty blue toward the far horizon. The steel-white of Lake Amadeus comes into view—one of those countless "lakes" of central Australia that are so rarely watered and lie encrusted with a shimmering coat of salt. Occasionally a cattle or mission station will appear, set in a great loneliness, with "willy-willies" of red dust rising like small tornadoes into the sky. At length, seeming all the more incredible in this flat semidesert, the bizarre bulk of the Mount Olga range heaves itself into the pale blue.

Rising abruptly from the plain, with no foothills whatsoever, the mountain mass is 4.5 miles in breadth and soars at its highest peak to 1,500 feet above the plain. Dull red in color, it most resembles from a distance a monstrous assembly of crouching elephants huddled one against the other. Though undeniably impressive, it has a nightmare grandeur which is accentuated when the pilot weaves between the huge congested domes and sinister curved precipices. It is with some relief that the traveler flies on to even more peculiar Ayers Rock. For though this is not so large as the Olgas—being about one mile across at its broadest, five miles in circumference and 1,100 feet high—it has an unforgettably impressive grandeur. Sheer from the flat, arid soil, this vast red monolith, the largest in the world, rises like a lonely monument to the eternity of time and to the insignificance of mankind's brief spell upon this planet.

These mountains were first discovered in 1872, and even today geologists are uncertain as to the origin of the two isolated conglomerate masses. To the far north and south of them are ranges of a different composition, and the theory is that the monoliths constitute the debris, consolidated by weather throughout millennia, of great ranges which in this vast time have been otherwise entirely denuded from the land. Another theory, much disputed, is that they are enormous meteorites.

From the ground, Ayers Rock is even more impressive. The sides of the rock are nearly vertical, and even in parts overhanging. The top is a smooth, unbroken ovoid, but the north face is fretted by deep potholes, believed to have been caused by centuries of weathering. On the northwest corner, there is a long, curved slab, or pillar, 200 feet in height, which is joined to the rock at its top and base but is separate from it for most of its height, so that daylight can be seen between the pillar and the rock. According to the aborigines, this is an effigy of the kind of kangaroo their legendary ancestors once hunted.

THE aborigines, to whom the rock is sacred, are indeed much in evidence, for about its base there may be found ceremonial caves decorated with magical frescoes and still used for initiations. Even Europeans have been sufficiently impressed by the grandeur of the monolith to protest against proposals that a funicular railway be erected to its summit. It can be climbed on foot, but this is perilous without a guide and is discouraged, since deaths have already occurred.

The aircraft sets off again to visit the cattle stations on its return journey. For in the outback, where roads are few and distances enormous, the stations depend on the rural air service for mail and passenger transportation and for some goods. All cattle stations now have their own airstrips, but these are often primitive, and sometimes the pilot has to fly in low to chase off the cattle or the wallabies that are browsing on its uneven surface. When the plane rattles to a halt, it is etiquette to get out and talk, for yours may be the first new face the station dwellers have seen in weeks. Sometimes the plane is greeted by bronzed, lean-eyed stockmen;

or by a "jackeroo," or student cattleman, with the broad, battered hat that distinguishes the outback character from the city dweller; or by an aloof aboriginal truck driver, with a solemn "lubra," or aboriginal woman, perched on the cargo behind him.

An outback cattle station is not unlike many American-style ranches. The homesteads are modest and utilitarian, and the life there is hard and lonely, especially for the women. The stations may be enormous, extending over hundreds or even thousands of square miles, the pasture is poor, and the cattle are often reduced to eating shrubs and trees like the mulga. Despite artesian boring, drought is a constant menace, and the railheads or roads to which cattle must be driven are often hundreds of miles away. It is therefore not surprising that big meat-exporting companies now own most of the stations, which they run through managers, for in this rugged region small, privately owned stations would not be viable.

It is not too much to say that aircraft and radio have made the development of all northern Australia possible. Radio is used for communication between stations, for providing centrally broadcast lessons for the children, and for summoning help in case of need. When illness occurs, help is given by the Flying Doctor Service, which was inaugurated by the Reverend John Flynn, a Presbyterian minister, in 1928. In those days the Service used rickety D.H.50 biplanes, and Flynn and his pioneers were summoned by primitive radios whose generators were operated by foot pedals. Today there are 12 main medical posts, each with a resident doctor and pilot. Each covers a radius of 400 miles, so that two million square miles, or two thirds of the continent, are served by the Flying Doctors.

But the Northern Territory's future is not entirely agricultural. Gold and copper are mined at Tennant Creek and uranium at Rum Jungle, and huge bauxite deposits have been found on the Gove Peninsula in the northeast. And this material progress threatens the survival of the chief reserves of the tribal aborigines, which are mostly in Arnhem Land and the islands adjacent to the coast. These reserves cannot be entered by whites except by special permission, but when bauxite or uranium is discovered there, the permission is soon forthcoming. As the miners delve and their machinery clangs on the Gove Peninsula, the booming, rhythmical notes of the famous aboriginal trumpet, the five-foot *didjeridoo*, will doubtless become more melancholy and soon be silenced.

The largest state of the country, and the only one that extends all the way from north to south, is Western Australia, with an area of 975,920 square miles, or almost one third of the whole continent. But its population is only 800,000, of whom more than half live in and about the capital, Perth. The reason is that huge areas of the state are deserts extending for hundreds of miles—though these "deserts" are not great expanses of sand, but a varied country of low ranges and shallow gullies filled with huge boulders, and with occasional clumps of spiky spinifex, desert acacia and the so-called pale ghost gum trees. The temperature rises to 120° F., but after the rare short rains a profusion of wild flowers bursts into momentary life and the sky is thick with vivid parrots and, high in formation flights, white or black cockatoos.

Among the rare fertile regions of the state is the northwestern area of the Kimberley Mountains, which are watered by short but copious rivers. Chief of these is the Ord, on which catchments to irrigate the countryside have been built. This is a cattle area, and since the distances are too great to allow the animals to be herded to seaports without their losing

THE ENORMOUS, VACANT OUTBACK

Australians use the term "outback" to describe the vast and rugged inland regions of their country. The word is a survivor of some curious and seemingly contradictory Australian terminology. For example, when an Australian reached the very interior of the continent, he used to say he was "right outside." Similarly, a man from the outback would say he was going "inside" when he headed for a city, which was likely to be on the coast. The most rugged and remote regions are still often described by the phrase "back-of-beyond." The primary reasons why this hinterland is so empty of man and his works are deficiencies in the soil and the scarcity of water. Even in areas where enough rain falls, precipitation is unpredictable. As a result, crop farming in the outback is all but impossible, and since pasturage is extremely thin, cattle and sheep stations must be of enormous size to contain enough forage for their herds or flocks.

weight, an "air beef" scheme is being introduced whereby the cattle are slaughtered and frozen on the stations and airlifted to the coast. There, in ports like Wyndham and Derby, they are shipped south to Perth or directly overseas. Perhaps the most peculiar, and certainly the most Asian, township in Australia is Broome, once a center for pearl fishing, and largely inhabited by Japanese and Malays who still use it as a base for operations in the Indian Ocean.

This area has some of the strangest of flora and fauna. The baobab tree uses its grotesquely swollen base to store water against the droughts. The bower-bird of the Ord River decorates its nest with any scintillating object it can plunder—broken glass, bottle tops, even coins. There are crocodiles, both fresh water and salt, and the wild pig is hunted in the hills. So are the kangaroos, which are shot, since on the cattle and sheep stations there may be eight times as many hungry kangaroos as sheep.

THE capital, Perth, on the meandering Swan River, is 12 miles from the Indian Ocean, but built-up areas join it to its harbor city, Fremantle, the last port of call for vessels sailing from Australia to the west. Perth's isolation will be understood from the fact of its being 1,700 miles away from the nearest other state capital, Adelaide. But though small—perhaps because it is—Perth is the most charming capital in the country, with the size of a big city yet with a sense, which all the other state capitals have lost, of still belonging to its huge hinterland. People in Perth are touchy about themselves and their state because they feel that its interests are sacrificed to the more populous regions of the east, and that most visitors are content to visit Australia and neglect its largest and wildest state.

Inland to the east are Kalgoorlie and Coolgardie, which achieved their earliest fame as flourishing gold-mining towns. Today Coolgardie is almost a ghost city, with baroque buildings abandoned from more prosperous days, but Kalgoorlie is still thriving, producing $19.9 million worth of gold a year. Beyond lies one of the loneliest regions in Australia, the Great Nullarbor Plain, which extends, like a terrestrial sea, 350 miles from west to east and 150 miles inland from the sea waters of the huge bay called the Great Australian Bight. So changeless is this enormous plateau that the transcontinental railway which crosses it runs straight as a die for 300 miles—the longest even stretch of track of any railroad in the world.

After this desolation, it is pleasant to reach the country's most elegant city, Adelaide, the capital of South Australia. This state is the third largest, extending for 380,000 square miles, and more than 60 per cent of its population of nearly a million lives in the capital city. This is partly because much of the state's outback is desert interspersed with huge salt lakes. But elsewhere the state is fertile, with cattle in the north, sheep and wheat throughout the center, and near Adelaide the rich Barossa Valley, where some of Australia's finest wines are produced.

The cliché about Adelaide is that it is the "city of churches," and indeed the tone of the town is decorous and sedate. Adelaide "society" is far more closely knit than that of most state capitals, and the tone is set by old pastoralist families and by formidable ladies much addicted to copiously flowered hats who view all unfortunates born outside Adelaide with considerable reserve. But the city has real beauty, with the Torrens River dammed into artificial lakes, a generous green belt of parklands, and splendid perspectives, even from the city center, of the graceful surrounding hills.

FOR two weeks every two years haughty Adelaide lets down its well-tended hair when the international festival erupts in the tranquil city. In theory, one might think it the last place to welcome thousands of peculiar aliens and exotic artists, but Adelaide rises to the occasion with surprising fervor. Handsome girls pin flowers in visiting buttonholes at the airport, wine companies leave discreet gifts in hotel bedrooms for astonished Filipino dancers and Czech actors, and there is a veritable orgy of lavish private entertainment. For two weeks the citizens are subjected to a massive dose of culture in every conceivable art, and they stay the course bravely, turning out by the thousands for exhibitions, jazz concerts, avant-garde plays and late-night satirical reviews.

Industry is growing in the state, for there are rich iron deposits, and vast new steel mills are being erected. From Woomera, north of Adelaide, the Long Range Weapons Establishment launches guided missiles across the continent into the Western Australian deserts. The country's chief jewel, the opal, is mined at Coober Pedy and elsewhere; and though this is said to be an unlucky stone, it competes with stuffed koala bears and mass-produced "native boomerangs" in the gift shops of the capital.

IF it may be said that there are two Australias— that of the predominantly rural "outback" states and that of the densely populated southeastern coastal fringe—the contrast is best illustrated when the traveler leaves the huge territories of the west and enters the populous State of Victoria. For though this is the second-smallest state, with only 87,884 square miles, it has more than three million inhabitants, or a quarter of the population of the entire continent. The concentration of cities and of roads and railways here is far more intense than in any other state, for Victoria is well watered and the soil is fertile. Sheep stations, dairy farms and fruit orchards are abundant.

The capital city, Melbourne, has nearly two million people and is fast overtaking its great rival, Sydney. Indeed, in its heyday in the 19th Century, Melbourne was the country's largest city, and until the establishment of the federal capital at Canberra, it was the seat of the whole nation's Government. Melbourne seems very conscious of these past glories and confronts the world in a stately, dignified and slightly pompous posture. Thus, an absolute dogma of all Melbournians is that their city is one of noble and impressive grandeur. With the best will in the world it is rather hard for the visitor to see it quite this way, since it appears to him to consist of a gridiron of large, dull thoroughfares down which the north wind howls amid the clanking of obsolete electric trams. The river Yarra, to the impartial eye, is a small, turgid, murky stream. However, try saying all this in Melbourne!

Yet to be just, it should be said that the charms of this city need greater discovery than those of any other in the country. To begin with, one will find that its intellectual life is more intense and authentic than elsewhere, for the University of Melbourne is a premier seat of learning in the nation,

and the new Monash University bids fair to rival its achievements. And if one may find the city in general dull, there are cultural oases of enormous interest, of which the chief is the new National Art Gallery and Cultural Center. This is the work of Roy Grounds, one of the most dynamic architects— and indeed personalities—in Australia. A fierce, amiable and immensely competent man, who resembles somewhat a displaced pirate, Roy Grounds has long startled the conservative Melbournians by the eclectic daring of his private buildings. The Cultural Center will no doubt be his masterwork.

But really the beauty of the state is found in its great variety of bush scenery—the thick gum forests of the east, the rich agricultural pastures of the Murray Basin to the north, and to the west the famous Wimmera, where much of the country's finest wool and wheat is grown—though some of these areas are frequently threatened by devastation from "bush fires." In extreme contrast to the arid austerity of the northern cattle stations, the Wimmera still sustains the traditional pastoralist existence of Australia's earlier days. Here one may see a station life that is the nearest thing in Australia to that of a landed aristocracy: the big house of the pastoralist, the nearby village for his manager, drovers and, in the season, shearers, and the wide acres lined with laboriously built rock barriers that enclose the huge herds of docile sheep. The graziers also make a lot of money, which enables them to keep cars and horses for their handsome children, to take part in rural "gymkhanas," or country fairs, and to descend on the brash cities for the Royal Easter Show with the air of those who enshrine the real virtues of Australia.

TO the south, 150 miles across the Bass Strait, lies the "Island State" of Tasmania, which is the smallest, with a mere 26,215 square miles. Tasmanians (they do not wish to be called Australians) are rather exclusive people and refer somewhat disdainfully to the vast neighboring continent as "the mainland." The population is only 360,000, of which that of the capital, Hobart, comprises about one third. This is a city with an exquisite setting on innumerable estuaries of the river Derwent, and with grandiose Mount Wellington rising abruptly 4,166 feet above the town. But truth to tell, Hobart itself is a rather meager, melancholy place despite its great natural beauty, with fingers of dull if pretty suburbs extending tentatively into the surrounding foothills.

To those who are seeking some remnants of Australia's recent historic past, Tasmania is the state to visit, for there are many signs of the convict settlements and of the early Georgian buildings of the penal colony. Although much of the island is gracious and fertile, with rich fruit orchards and small sheep farms, parts of the west coast, despite the smallness of the island, are still among the wildest and most impenetrable regions of the country, and in these fastnesses that uninviting beast, the Tasmanian wolf, may still be encountered.

Before proceeding northward from Victoria, we must pause at the Australian Capital Territory, which occupies some 910 square miles carved out of New South Wales, with an additional enclave of 28 square miles on the sea, which contains the naval college, at nearby Jervis Bay. Its major city, Canberra, the federal capital, came into existence at the time of the federation in 1901 as a compromise in a dispute between Melbourne and Sydney as to which rival metropolis should be chief city of the new nation. Canberra's population today is some 79,000, and a third of these are civil servants.

After the agreement was made to build Canberra, 10 years passed before much was done about it, though a superb site of handsome ranges surrounding the basin of the Molonglo River was selected. In 1911 the world's architects were invited to an international competition to design the city, and out of 137 entries the first prize went to an American, Walter Burley Griffin. Although Griffin was eyed suspiciously by the Australians, the choice turned out to be a blessing in disguise, for in the American the young nation secured an artist of outstanding talent who had been a disciple of Louis Sullivan's in Chicago and an associate of Frank Lloyd Wright's. In 1913, Burley Griffin arrived in Australia and was appointed Federal Capital Director.

Griffin's original ground plan, which with unfortunate modifications is still substantially that of Canberra today, called for a series of interlocking circles and hexagons set on a triangle of three great triumphal avenues. In the center, there was to be a series of artificial lakes, and the buildings, both public and private, were to be zoned as to function and kept on a scale appropriate to the natural setting. But by 1920, when he had completed only his main avenues and roads, Griffin, who found himself the victim of every species of obstruction by bureaucrats with no knowledge of architecture whatever, was dismissed from the project and retired into private practice.

However, although they got rid of Griffin, the city fathers of Canberra fortunately retained many of his ideas, so that the layout of the city remains one of noble simplicity, while some of the buildings, like the graceful, arcaded Civic Center, preserve the core of Griffin's ideal of unpretentious dignity. But elsewhere crude office blocks have been allowed to throw his whole scheme out of scale, and many of the suburbs are so shapelessly sprawling that Canberra has been unkindly called "sixteen suburbs in search of a city." The federal Parliament House is a meaningless box unworthy of a national capital, though everyone fortunately realizes this, and a new one is to be built. Of greater architectural merit are the simple and functional buildings of the Australian National University, and the huge inverted saucer of the Academy of Sciences,

---

IMPROVING THE CATTLE BREED

The first cattle brought to Australia were of the Zebu breed, called Brahman in the U.S., which were acquired by early settlers when their ships stopped at the Cape of Good Hope. A rugged beast, able to withstand a hot and arid climate, the Zebu was well adapted to the rough conditions existing in the early colonies. So were the small Indian cattle introduced in 1791. But as farms became more settled, these humped and hardy kine were often crossbred with, or supplanted by, more profitable beef and dairy cattle from England. English Shorthorns were successfully imported in 1825, and in 1826 the bull Billy and the cows Matchless and Beauty became the first of Australia's Herefords. Further importation and crossbreeding have continued in this century, with some farmers favoring hornless cattle, which are less likely to bruise one another and spoil their beef for freezing. And in 1952 breeding came full circle when the King Ranch of Texas sent to Australia some Santa Gertrudis cattle, a breed developed by crossing Shorthorns with Zebus.

---

designed by Roy Grounds. Canberra has already cost $450 million and will undoubtedly cost many millions more. For whereas, until quite recently, it was a transients' city to which civil servants came reluctantly from the big state capitals, it has now the most rapid population increase of any Australian city. The staffs of the armed services have joined the diplomats, academics and Government servants in making Canberra an authentic federal center with a high concentration of enterprising brains.

New South Wales, with four million people, is the most populous state of the Commonwealth, although, with its 309,432 square miles, it is only the fourth largest. The capital, Sydney, with 2.5 million people, is the country's largest city, with more than half the population of the state and one fifth that of the whole continent. Its inhabitants are inordinately proud of Sydney, and the city may thus be judged by the highest international standards.

IT must at once be said that Sydney is not quite so remarkable as its loyal populace supposes. The celebrated and indispensable Harbor Bridge, though a striking engineering achievement, has, apart from its size, no particular beauty. Nor is the renowned harbor as sensational as those, for instance, of Rio or Naples. Nevertheless, it is a superb natural anchorage, with a variety of deep-sea inlets that penetrate far into the city on both shores. Its architectural surroundings are on the whole mediocre, yet the whole panorama of its bays, coves and estuaries has immense variety and vivacity, and the harbor itself, when seen in certain lights and from many places, is so exquisite that all the human attempts to ruin it have not yet succeeded in destroying its great natural beauty.

Historic central Sydney is quite small, with narrow streets leading down to the Circular Quay, where Governor Phillip first landed (though no one is sure of the exact spot). From here ferries set off for points all around the harbor, and from these boats its beauty and extent can be better realized than from anywhere on the land. On the farther side of the quay, at Bennelong Point, is the location of Sydney's tribute to the 20th Century: its fabled Opera House. On a stunning site, jutting right out into the harbor, there will arise one of the most remarkable buildings in the Southern Hemisphere. Designed by a young Dane, Joern Utzon, whose drawings were chosen from among 217 international entries, the Opera House will contain four halls and theaters of various sizes surmounted by a series of gigantic shells of precast concrete rising at the highest point to 216 feet, or 20 stories of a conventional building. As an exercise in the imaginative capture of space on a splendid scale, and as a cultural center worthy of a great city, the Opera House must be commended. But the cost, whose estimate increases annually and now stands at $39 million, and the repeated postponements of the finishing date make Sydneysiders wonder. However, they support the project, if not with all their hearts, by subscribing to a state lottery to finance it.

Rising above the harbor in the center of the city is a fine green expanse of park, and nearby there survive buildings of Australia's first master architect, Francis Howard Greenway. Greenway was a convict whom Governor Macquarie pardoned to embellish the growing city, and his exquisite St. James' Church, built in 1819, is a precious link between Sydney's bustling present and its cruel past. Another surprise is to find, in some of the outlying districts, terraces of early-19th Century houses decorated with delicate metalwork in what is called the "cast-iron vernacular" style. Metal brought out as ballast in the early sailing ships was used by local craftsmen to ornament buildings with balconies and pillars in this attractive and fanciful baroque.

BUT what redeems Sydney is its bubbling vivacity and animation. Its climate is delightful, with an average of 342 sunny days a year, though there is a boisterous Pacific wind. To see a spectacle like the start of the Sydney-to-Hobart yacht race, in which hundreds of escorting craft lace the glittering estuaries with a flock of speeding sails, is to forget the man-made ugliness that mars the beauty of the harbor. Not far inland, there is the rugged splendor of the Blue Mountains, and fronting the Pacific, Sydney's great glory, the superb string of surfing beaches where so many Sydneysiders live throughout the summer.

The state itself, though rich in sheep, beef, wheat and dairy farms, is specially noted for industrial and mining complexes like the steel city of New-castle and the silver, lead and zinc mines of Broken Hill. The most famous enterprise of all is the Snowy Mountains Scheme in the ranges south of Canberra, which was begun in 1949 and will cost an estimated $892 million by the time it is completed in 1975. This Scheme has the double object of irrigation and the generating of hydroelectric power, and a sub-sidiary aim of helping develop a vast national park around the country's highest mountain, Mount Kosciusko. The chief feature of the Scheme is the joining of the Snowy River waters, through tunnels beneath the mountains, with those of the Murray and Murrumbidgee Rivers. The total area involved is 3,000 square miles of mountainous country, in which has been created a great artificial storage lake, Eucumbene, with a capacity of nearly four million acre-feet of water. There are to be eight large and many smaller dams; 100 miles of tunnels, often 3,000 feet below the surface; more than 80 miles of aqueducts; and 10 hydroelectric power stations, many of them hundreds of feet underground. When completed, the Scheme will produce more than three million kilowatts of peak-load power and nearly two million acre-feet of additional waters which will irri-gate some 1,000 square miles and be carried into the neighboring states of Victoria and South Australia.

THE administrative headquarters of the project are at Cooma, a boom town where one almost expects to meet Hopalong Cassidy, since it has a decided frontier atmosphere. Three fourths of the labor force working on the Scheme is made up of im-migrants, and the flags of all the peoples who have contributed fly proudly in Cooma's central square. Light industry is already appearing, forestry is being developed, and since to see "the Snowy" is a tourist must, thousands of Australians come south from Canberra to admire what their adventurous country-men have achieved.

Going north to the "Sunshine State" of Queens-land, we return to a predominantly outback region. For Queensland, with 670,500 square miles, is the second-largest state but has a population of only 1.5 million, of whom more than a third live in the capital, Brisbane. This is a rather dilapidated city on a winding river of the same name, and is tucked away in the southeast corner of the state close to the New South Wales border, as if alarmed by its huge tropical hinterland to the north. Many of its older dwellings stand elegantly on stilts, having been de-signed for maximum coolness in the days before air conditioning. Nearby on the coast is the most remarkable series of beaches in the whole country, known as the Gold Coast, beside whose 20 miles of sands some 150,000 holidaymakers occupy a sort of mammoth fun fair of garish chalets and motels.

For Queensland is the state to which sun seekers come in winter, and all up its long Pacific coast are smaller cities of great tropical beauty, often border-ing on thick, rain-soaked forests with a deep, rich ochered soil. From these ports the visitor can explore the enormous extent of the Great Barrier Reef, in whose hundreds of miles of multicolored corals swim myriad tropical fish which may be examined from glass-bottomed boats or, by those who do not fear sharks, stonefish, barracuda and giant clams, by skin diving.

In this hot climate, there grow sugar cane, pineap-ples and tobacco, but the mainstay of the state is cattle, and there are sheep stations toward the some-what cooler south. Queensland is rich in raw materi-als, with copper, lead and zinc at the big inland mines of Mount Isa, uranium at Mary Kathleen and huge bauxite deposits on the Cape York Peninsula. But the most sensational recent discovery is that of oil and natural gas at Moonie, and oil is now being piped 200 miles to Brisbane. Indeed, it is impossible to visit Queensland without sensing that this state, the most attractive of all, is on the verge of a star-tling industrial and agricultural development.

ACROSS the Torres Strait and to the northeast are the Australian-administered United Na-tions trust territories of New Guinea and Nauru, with a total population of 1.5 million, of which about 15,000 are Europeans. Australia has jurisdic-tion over several more islands in the Pacific, while in the far south the nation lays bold claim to 2.5 mil-lion square miles of Antarctica, though this is not internationally recognized. In actuality, Australians do not get very excited about overseas territories. Small wonder: for they have a continent so huge and splendid to develop for themselves.

John Spiers (center), his father (left) and a stockman brew lunchtime "billy tea" on the Spierses' South Australia sheep station.

A Lonely Life Bringing Rewards and Hardships

Although four fifths of Australia's population lives in cities and towns, a sheep grazier or cattleman on one of the vast "stations" in the interior is more typically the true Aussie. Ideally, the station owner can combine hard work with the amenities of civilization. However, on a station in the outback, where vegetation is sparse and rain infrequent, a man like John Spiers *(above and pages 46-51)* faces isolation and sometimes heartbreaking drought. Only in the fertile regions, like the area where Michael White operates his cattle station *(pages 52-55)*, do conditions make possible a prosperous and comfortable life.

DRAFTING SHEEP, John Spiers *(foreground)* separates them before clipping their matted wool. The Mern Merna station, a name taken from an aboriginal term meaning "permanent water," grazes 8,000 sheep and 300 cattle on 150 square miles.

RIDING HERD, stockman Ian Stephenson musters a mob of sheep *(left)*, driving them toward the stockyards. Because the average annual rainfall is only nine inches in this area, 10 acres are needed for grazing one sheep on the sparsely vegetated land.

47

AN OUTBACK FAMILY, the John Spierses lead a rugged, demanding life in their determination to draw a livelihood from the arid land

PLANTING VEGETABLES, Mrs. John Spiers and her youngest child, two-year-old Mary Lou, work in the garden near their home. The station provides its own meat, and Mrs. Spiers goes only once a week to the nearest town, 19 miles away, for green vegetables, and even less often to Adelaide for staples.

REPAIRING A WINDMILL, John Spiers examines the blades at a water bore *(opposite)* while his stockman climbs the ladder to join him. Since the sheep drink all of their water at bore tanks, when a windmill is broken the sheep must be moved several miles to another paddock until the mill is fixed.

RIDING THEIR PONY in the stockyard, four of the Spiers children take their turns on Bonny *(right).* The children spend much of their time with animals as part of their everyday chores. Even two-year-old Mary Lou performs a regular task on the station: she feeds the chickens and collects their eggs.

SUPPERTIME brings all six of the Spiers children to the table *(right)*. Mrs. Spiers serves, left to right, Peter, Anne, Mary Lou, Richard, Jane and Phillip. The children are the fifth generation of the Spiers family to live on the Mern Merna station.

LESSONS BY RADIO provide schooling *(opposite)* for the Spiers children. As their governess coaches the others, Anne, six, talks by radio to a teacher of the School of the Air, which conducts daily classes from a central location in South Australia.

QUIET MOMENT at the day's end gives John and Pam Spiers a chance for relaxation *(below)*. As Pam knits, John sets up his projector to show eight-millimeter home movies. Picnics, family sings and personal hobbies help pass the evenings.

DRIVING HIS CATTLE into the stockyards, Michael White, the owner of the Belltrees station in New South Wales, holds a whip in either hand. Five thousand head of Aberdeen Angus cattle and 10,000 Merino sheep graze on the 20,000 acres at Belltrees, which has been in the White family since 1842. Modern chemical fertilizers have helped make the land rich.

the means to support a round of pleasures

ASSIGNING WORK, Michael White assembles his stockmen in the morning under a tree in front of the station office building. Work assignments have been given out here for 100 years.

CLOSING A PRESS, White and a hired hand secure a calf within the wooden device before branding the animal. Using the press reduces injuries to stockmen and speeds the process.

WATCHING AN AUCTION with agents, buyers and other station owners *(right)*, White *(center)* surveys the cattle about to be sold at a weekly cattle and sheep sale in nearby Scone.

PREPARING DINNER, Judy White makes a mocha icebox cake while her youngest child, Scott, plays alongside. She does all of her own cooking but has full-time help for housework.

ENTERTAINING FRIENDS at a formal dinner, Michael and Judy White preside at opposite ends of the table in the Belltrees dining room. Most of the guests live on neighboring stations.

RIDING TO SCHOOL, Anthony White, seven *(left)*, and his brother Peter, five, approach the one-room school which has served local primary and high-school children since 1912.

PICNICKING WITH RELATIVES, Judy White *(in striped jersey)* serves a large gathering of in-laws who have come to enjoy a Sunday meal on the Whites' gently rolling property.

Miners in Mount Isa meet for a drink at a beer garden on a Sunday morning. A copper-mining town in Queensland, Mount Isa has many

"New Australians," as a third of the miners are immigrants.

4

A Breezy, Unpredictable People

IN his poem "The True Discovery of Australia," James McAuley, the nation's eminent poet, has described his fellow countrymen in these laconic lines:

> *The men are brave, contentious, ignorant;*
> *The women very much as one expects.*

How true is this? Certainly the Australian male is tough—very tough—and in appearance lean-eyed, hatchet-jawed, relaxed and slightly ungainly. The girls generally run in two types—either a rather stringy, small-breasted, leggy girl with a sun-baked complexion, or else one with a large-hipped figure and an easy grace of posture. Both sexes look athletic, purposeful and healthy; yet each may be said to lack style and glamor. For this is still a male society in which women are respected, certainly—and indeed pursued—yet treated with an almost masculine camaraderie, so that the girls tend to be boyish: frank and kindly, but lacking mystery and romance. Among older generations, that formidable figure, the large, competent, bossy Australian Mum, and her wiry, rugged consort Dad, bear witness to the country's strength of character.

Temperamentally, both the men and the women are friendly, humorous and sardonic; but underneath this affable exterior, there are undertones of both sensitivity and violence. The frenetic performance of Australian warriors and athletes has often been recorded, and this tendency can reveal itself, at moments, in ordinary social life. Australians, so lackadaisical and cordial, can suddenly *explode;* and when they do, the spectacle is alarming. Thus, in his relations with Australians, the visitor may find himself passing rapidly through three stages. Initially, he will be welcomed with open arms—embraced almost too closely, and too quickly, for his comfort. Stage two comes when, for some reason inexplicable to the visitor, he touches the Aussie on some raw and secret nerve that arouses a swift and disproportionate animosity, whereupon the visitor is fixed with a malevolent, baleful eye. Then stage three is reached, in which the stranger is taken utterly for granted and has become part of the local scenery. (As the reader may well imagine, it is vital to pass as quickly as possible from stage one to stage three.)

IT is very difficult to impress Australians. Perhaps a champion athlete can do it, but certainly no one else. Any attempt to "pull rank" is resented and will get you absolutely nowhere, for this society, despite increasing variations in the wealth of individuals, does remain, in its forms at any rate, egalitarian. Yet to the dogma of social equality, there are important reservations. The national myth is one of "mateship," a tradition born in pioneering days, when social solidarity, in adverse conditions, was the most prized virtue. But today Australians live in huge towns and are no longer poor; and though the cult of "mateship" has remained, and may still be valid in rural regions and among urban workingmen, in the cities generally it has more form than substance. The patrician landowners and the industrialists who meet at the exclusive Melbourne Club may pay public lip service to equality, but they do not believe in it in terms of power and deeds.

An unattractive aspect of the egalitarian spirit is that Australians are reluctant to give credit where it is due. A man of achievement is accorded a publicity

value but not much else. For Australians are great "knockers," and a man of high talent may often be pursued by a kind of envious rancor. This may account for the remarkable absence of heroes in Australia. Athletes—yes, perhaps. But who can name even a dozen distinguished citizens on whom their compatriots have bestowed unreserved esteem? Hundreds of Australians of enormous gifts and competence are regarded by the populace with no awe whatsoever. On the other hand, what a blessed relief to escape from the restricting toils of pomposity and hierarchy that entangle other nations. You can approach most Australians, however high their status, with the certainty of a ready, cordial hearing. And though Australian manners may lack formality, they are easy and unaffected: the visitor is greeted with a courteous familiarity.

There is also the dichotomy between the life-loving, outward-giving spirit of this country and a deep streak of puritanism. Thus the sexual lives of young Australians seem harmonious and permissive; but in the public sector, there is often a display of ludicrous prudishness. Take, for example, censorship. Many books are arbitrarily banned, and recently the State of Victoria worked itself into a frenzy as to whether its citizens would be polluted by the sale of Mary McCarthy's novel *The Group.* A public exhibition of nude paintings can still arouse paroxysms of ire among moralizing politicians.

FROM his first arrival, the visitor will hear the celebrated Australian accent. This is thought by some to be hideous, comical and not unlike a sort of bastard Cockney. Now, the point about accents is that they are things everybody is afflicted with—except for oneself! Everyone who speaks English has an accent of one kind or another, and to anyone with an acute ear, the comparison with Cockney is absurd. Cockney is lilting, slurred and lively. Australian is nasal, flat and expressive. What most strikes the hearer is how perfectly fitted this tongue is to the sardonic, speculative Aussie temperament, and to deny eloquence to Australians is to fail to grasp their art of deadpan understatement.

One curiosity, however, is that while Australia is almost as large as the United States, there is not the wide variety of accents to be found in America. Even

Australians admit that a Sydneysider cannot readily distinguish, by ear alone, a man from Perth, though he comes from thousands of miles away. Perhaps the reasons are that in the U.S., a much older country, there has been time for regional accents to develop and that climatic variations—which may well help to determine accent—have had far greater effect.

It is not surprising that this new accent accompanies a new vocabulary—usually words of a mildly pejorative flavor. Thus a *bludger* is a parasitic fellow who, if he does not stick to his *lurk,* or racket, may soon be in a *yike,* or trouble, in which case his situation will be *crook,* or disagreeable. *Bodgies* and *widgies* are near-delinquent boys and girls. A more general term for a girl is *sheila,* and when you go out to look for one in your best *togs,* or clothes, you hope she will be *beaut* and perhaps even indulge with you in some *grog* (liquor) or *plonk* (wine), if you offer to *shout* her, or pay for it. And so on. There are hundreds of these pungent terms, casually colorful, and used chiefly to suggest a tone of amiable, tolerant contempt.

TO consider Australians in more general terms, they are a young nation, with 40 per cent of the population under 21, a birth rate of 23 per 1,000 and the greatest fertility in the 20 to 24 age group. Yet even so, large families are still exceptional, and in this factor—together with a small over-all population—lies the central problem of Australian social and political life, that of population growth.

Although Australia is not so rich, in terms of soil, rainfall and raw materials, as its vast size might suggest, there can be little doubt that it could support a much larger population than its present 11 million—and do so without lowering its general living standards. This is particularly so now that the country is fast becoming industrialized. And in the external political sphere, Australians feel that their minute population is a constant provocation to overpopulated Asian nations to turn envious eyes upon this empty land.

What population *could* Australia support? Theories about this range from 20 million to as much as 40 million, but most experts agree that the present population is inadequate on military, social and economic grounds. Critics of population increase

maintain that it is useless to hope to rival Asia's millions: for even if Australia doubled its population, it would still be negligible by comparison with its nearest neighbor, Indonesia, let alone India or China. Does not a small population make certain the high living standard? Is a large internal market so important to Australian business, since Australia is, and always must be, an exporting country?

But those who speak against increase are now in a minority, and since World War II Australia has embarked on a policy of massive immigration under which more than two million people have entered the country in the past two decades, principally from Europe. Immigration offices have been set up in several countries; cheap, subsidized sea passages granted; jobs provided (though not always the jobs the immigrants wanted); and accommodations furnished, initially, in Government hostels. After five years in the country, the assisted immigrant can, if he wishes, take out naturalization papers.

To increase a population by almost one fifth in so short a time was a bold and difficult undertaking. In the first place, Australians were not, a generation ago, a welcoming people to the foreigner: xenophobia was general, and ignorance of the outside world was considerable. The Government wisely launched a program of national education and insisted that the newcomers should be called not by the unflattering terms Australians reserved for aliens, but simply "New Australians." But at the same time, there arose a second, even graver problem: should immigration be confined to Europeans or should Asians also at last be allowed in?

THE "White Australia Policy" is supported by most of the population and by all political parties (except for the Communist), though everyone, in the modern international climate that condemns racialism, wishes this policy were not called openly what in fact it is. At one time, to enforce it, an ingenious device was used—a triumph of bureaucratic legerdemain. There was no overt questioning of the prospective immigrant as to race: he was merely asked to take, on arrival, a "dictation test" in *any* European language selected by the examiner. Thus, even if the hapless immigrant knew two, 10 or, for that matter, 100 tongues, one that he did not know could always be chosen for the test. Since 1958 this pretense has been abandoned, and permission to enter the country is accorded arbitrarily by the Minister for Immigration—who does not have to justify his decision. What this means in effect is that persons of European stock are allowed to settle and Afro-Asians are not.

There are thus to be found in Australia the following non-European groups: the aborigines; the native-born Chinese minority; Melanesians from islands administered by Australia; Asian students admitted under foreign-aid plans; and transients such as diplomats, businessmen, artists and merchant seamen. The total non-European population is less than 1 per cent.

WHAT are the advantages of this situation? Firstly, of course, that Australia has a more or less homogeneous racial structure. Next—and this point is often missed by liberal critics of the Policy— that Australians are the only people of European origin who, living in a torrid climate, have done most of their own manual work. The temptation, a century ago and later, to introduce cheap coolie labor on a vast scale must have been enormous.

A curious consequence of the Policy is that in Australia, thanks to the very fact that there is no color problem (unless we include that of the aborigines), racial relations with visiting men of color are harmonious. There is no hostility to an Afro-Asian because he is in no way felt to be a menace.

But what are the disadvantages? They are part political, part social. There is no doubt that, in the international sphere, the Policy irritates Australia's Asian neighbors. With some of these countries, like the Philippines, Australia is allied; while another, Indonesia, is its closest neighbor. Of course, it may be that these Asian nations close their own frontiers to immigrants; it may be that they have not fully exploited, with their vaster populations, their own potential riches; it may be that Asians would not want to come in large numbers to Australia, even if they could. Nevertheless, the Policy is an obstacle to the extension of Australian trade and influence in Asia and the Pacific.

The social disadvantages are more subtle. By almost completely excluding Asians, Australia cuts itself off from the possibility of bringing in talents that the country badly needs. On the one hand, Australia eagerly seeks skilled European immigrants, most of whom, in conditions of increasing European prosperity, wish to remain at home. On the other, it absolutely bars Asians whose labor might be of great value. The feeling is thus growing—though it is still very much a minority feeling—that selected Asian immigrants should be admitted.

A further disadvantage of the Policy is that Australians, racially speaking, live in a sort of vacuum. There is no other subtropical country one can think of where a racial problem—which, with nationalism, is perhaps the major problem of our times—does not exist. By shutting their doors firmly to Asians, Australians have achieved social harmony at the expense of a deeper understanding of the racial problems that surround them.

In the long run, any change of policy will doubtless be based on four key considerations. Would Asian immigration diminish living standards? Would it encourage economic development? Would it harm social integration? And would it endanger national security? If Asian immigration were controlled, the answer to the first question would seem to be "No," to the second "Yes" and to the final two "Perhaps." This is a hard decision, on which it would be irresponsible for non-Australians to pass judgment, since they do not have to live out the consequences of making it.

IN any event, when a target of about 100,000 immigrants annually was adopted a year after World War II, it was confined to Europeans. Of the total numbers who have reached Australia under this program, some 50 per cent have come from the United Kingdom, 19 per cent from southern Europe (chiefly Italians), 10 per cent from the Slav countries (mostly Poles), and 14 per cent from the European North (especially Dutch and Germans). This means that many recent immigrants are of national stocks new to Australia, and also that, as a consequence of the total immigration during this century, one sixth of Australia's population today is not native-born.

In general terms, the White Australia Policy has worked surprisingly well. Many immigrants were dissatisfied with the jobs they were allocated and with the regimented accommodations, and many returned home (though many have come back to Australia again). On the other hand, the advantages to the immigrants have been considerable: a fine climate in many areas, a high living standard, in many cases new political liberties and—or so many optimistically thought—a relative freedom from the threat of the atom bomb. From the native Australian point of view, the value of the Policy lay in an increased labor force, the introduction of new skills and a greater diversification of the country's cultural life.

The immigrants most liked by the Australians are those from the northern part of Europe: Dutch, Scandinavians and Germans in particular. These nationals are felt to be energetic, reliable and loyal. The immigrants from southern Europe—Italian, Spanish, Greek and Yugoslav, for instance—are less accepted and admired. This is chiefly because the northerners are assimilated more easily than the southerners, who are likely to live and work in their own exclusive areas, not "muck in" with the native-born, and fail—especially among the older generations—to learn comprehensible English. Another objection is that the Roman Catholic minority is growing because of immigration. Australia is a predominantly Protestant country, and there is some resentment that Roman Catholics now number at least a quarter of the population and are increasing—as are, indeed, thanks to the new arrivals, the Greek Orthodox and Lutheran communities.

A further objection to some migrants—especially to those from southern Europe—is that the initial "screening" of them by the Australian authorities was so lax as to allow in gangsters and political undesirables. What also vexes the Australians is that a large proportion of the migrants do not, when they are able to do so, take out Australian citizenship, so that there are more than 400,000 aliens in Australia today. Indeed, a great many of them—the Greeks and Spaniards in particular—make it clear that their sole object in visiting Australia is to earn what they can and take it home.

But in reality, Australians accept this nonassimilation, since it is on the second generation of the immigrant population that the greatest hopes are placed. The parents, it is felt—whether they take out Australian papers or not—will remain tied emotionally to their distant homelands. But their children, born and raised in the new country, will be true Australians. This development indeed seems likely, for one can already meet young men and women of alien ancestry who are almost indistinguishable from the sons of the native-born.

Toward the largest group of all—those from the British Isles—the Australian attitude is on the whole unfavorable. It is admitted that there are able and skilled immigrants from the United Kingdom, and these have been welcomed. But of many it is said that they grumble, are idle and are afflicted by a sterile sense of superiority. Unfortunately, there seems much truth in these strictures, though Australian sensitivity may also partly account for them. The fact is that the heroic period of British worldwide emigration is now over—the period when the liveliest spirits of the country helped to people America, Africa and Australia itself. Today, the best potential British emigrant material is likely to want to stay home and share in Britain's own prosperity.

Here we may pause to ask how "British" Australia really is. To understand this we must realize that

---

AN AUSTRALIAN GLOSSARY

Bush. Any wooded area or region.
Gibber plains. Stony wastelands.
Larrikin. A young tough.
To barrack. To jeer or tease.
Grouse. Good, excellent.
Good on you. Term of approval sometimes used ironically.
Wowser. A strait-laced fanatic.
Willy-willy. A local windstorm.
Digger. Originally a miner, now an Australian soldier.
Hard yacker. Hard, exhausting work.
Shivoo. A spree or party.
Squib. A cowardly person.
Up a gum tree. In trouble, in a quandary.
Barney. A dispute or argument.
Drongo. A simpleton or fool.
Ratbag. An eccentric person.
Ropeable. Angry or irritated.
Sly-grog. Liquor sold illegally; also, a place where such liquor is sold.
Sticky-beak. An inquisitive person.
Jumbuck. A sheep.
The big smoke. Country term for the city.
To skite. To boast.
Picnic. A real mess.
Humpy. A small hut or building.
Tucker. Food or a meal.
To jack up. To abandon or reject.
To chyack. To tease or taunt.

the Australian concept of "Britishness" is entirely different from the native Englishman's. Superficially, there is an identity. Passports bear the words "British Passport," bank notes portray the faces, as national heroes, of English explorers and governors who were not native-born, and on public occasions the Union Jack is just as much in evidence as is the Australian flag. The countries share the same monarch; furthermore, the Governor-General and most of the state governors, although their function is largely decorative, are brought out from the United Kingdom. (Cynics aver the preference for Britons is because the populace is so disrespectful of authority that few native sons, however eminent, want the job or would even be able to perform its ceremonial duties with appropriate panache.)

BUT what does all this amount to in reality? To very little, for the attitude of Australians to the English is in fact highly equivocal. In a historic and largely sentimental sense, Australians may be attached to their British origins. Yet even before World War I, when England loomed large in the national consciousness, there was considerable hostility to the individual Briton. The word "Pommie," a term of vague origins used to describe a British immigrant, was never a kindly one, nor was it intended so to be. And ever since the collapse of British power in the East during and after World War II, and more recently since the shifts of British policy on applying to enter the Common Market, the alienation of Australia from Britain has been intensified. Thus, to Australians, the concept of "Britishness" is a purely local one. To be "British," in the Southwest Pacific, is a means of self-identification, a symbol of what differentiates Australians from Asians and Americans, but not one that binds them to the United Kingdom.

The fact is that Australians today are not much concerned with their origins, but more with finding and maintaining their own individual identity; and in some of their social customs we may seek for what is peculiar to their culture. What may first strike the observer is the contrast of prudence and rashness in the national temperament. Thus, so far as prudence goes, there is the remarkable proliferation of savings banks, even in suburban and rural areas, which make

Australians among the greatest savers on a per capita basis in the world; the high level of life insurance; the fact that no less than one fifth of the labor force is employed in Government service; and most of all, the absolute obsession with owning a house surrounded by a well-tended garden.

Now, the proliferation of suburbia is by no means a phenomenon exclusive to Australia, but in this country it takes on the most extreme forms. Australian cities, though not so large in population as those of Europe or America, are just as big in area because of the square miles of suburbs that stretch endlessly from the city centers, as if in denial of the great bush that lies beyond. These interminable rows of decorous, hygienic, nondescript bungalows seem in stark contrast to any vision one may have had of the Australians as a nation of individualists. More than 50 per cent of Australian homes are now owner-occupied, and this is increasing because of installment purchase and Government subsidy. To possess a suburban house, however cut off from the land, however inconveniently far from the central city, and however banal and monotonous in appearance, now seems part of the Australian dream.

YET one cannot conclude that this sameness of habitat induces a total conformity of spirit, since from these same uniform rows of streets emerge the athletes and warriors who have won Australia fame. And once outside the neat walls and cozy gardens, the rashness of the national temperament reasserts itself. Thus Australians are found to be inveterate gamblers, cool and extravagant in their wagers. Lotteries and horse racing are favorite diversions, but the special Australian contribution to the art is the national game of "two-up."

"Two-up schools" may be organized spontaneously wherever men forgather—on a building site, at a cattle station or near a country tavern. That the game is illegal does not deter the players, though lookouts are posted to warn against the intrusion of "the law." The men, in numbers ranging from a dozen to 200, gather in a circle facing inward. In charge of operations will be the "ringer," who takes a 10 per cent cut of all bets, acts as referee, and supplies strong-arm men who collect his percentage and prevent any disputes.

The ringer hands to any player who fancies himself an expert "spinner" a flat piece of wood on which are placed two penny coins—each usually burnished on the head side (which displays the monarch's features) and left dull on the tail (on which there is engraved a kangaroo). Before the spinner throws, the players lay wagers as to whether two heads or two tails will fall on the ground. (If the coins fall "odd"—a head and a tail—they must be spun again.) Wagers are individual between the gamblers—that is, you can bet, say, $100 on the throw with the man next to you, or if you wish to make a larger wager (sums of 100 Australian pounds—$224—or more are not infrequent in a prosperous "school") and cannot find one man to take all of your bet, you can split up the wager among as many players as will bet sums for the total you desire. All this is arranged with astonishing rapidity, the placing of bets of hundreds of pounds taking only a moment.

The ringer, a burly man of sharp wits and voluble authority, now calls on the spinner to throw the coins. The arm must be held at full length and the coins not projected skyward until the hand has risen above the head. When they are airborne, the coins must be seen to spin—that is, not just rise and fall flat—or a new throw will be called for. As soon as the coins hit the soil, the result is immediately visible through the different polish of the head and tail sides of the coins. Settlement is immediate, both between players and the ringer's assistants, and already new wagers are being placed on the next throw.

WHY is this game so immensely popular? Partly, no doubt, by the very fact that it is illegal, for this adds to its charm for the recalcitrant Aussie temperament. Partly because it is played out of doors and can be instantly and informally arranged in pauses between work or play. Partly because it is a sociable game—the tight-knit, excited crowd of a two-up school has a human warmth absent in the placing of individual bets with a bookmaker or an impersonal totalizator. Perhaps, most of all, because it is almost impossible to cheat in it. Sums wagered must be thrown down on the ground, and though ingenious spinners have sometimes succeeded in introducing double-sided coins, the risk is great, since everyone is watching, and the physical retribution visited on any fraud would be violent and sudden.

But it is perhaps in Australian drinking habits that a contrast of social customs may be seen most vividly: between inborn exuberance and severely imposed restraint. To begin with, there is still a strong temperance movement in Australia, whose political influence explains the restricted hours of drinking and the fact that drinking is chiefly limited to bars inside hotels. In two states, Victoria and South Australia, these close at 6 p.m., so that workers, knocking off at 5 or half past 5, have an hour or less in which to imbibe gallons. Chaos reigns in the beer-sodden, raucous hotel bars, and patrons stagger off, having drunk too much too fast, carrying bundles of bottles for home consumption. What is peculiar about this squalid saturnalia is that members of private clubs—which exist at all social levels—or anyone actually resident in a hotel may legally drink, if he wishes to, all around the clock. Luxury restaurants are also licensed at night. But public popular drinking in the hotels is forbidden, though in other states the doors do not slam until 10 p.m.

AUSTRALIANS are vertical, masculine drinkers. Here, in this country of Mediterranean climate, the social habits derived from northern Protestant Europe have survived. The drinkers mostly shut themselves off from the sunny streets into huge saloons, like banks, with nowhere to sit down—unless it be in the "lounge," the only part of a hotel to which one may normally take a reputable woman. Barmaids usually serve this masculine throng and are no doubt intended to induce, by their softening presence, a seemly standard of behavior. Jam-packed and raucous, the clients swill down enormous quantities of beer. But while no one could say the Australian pub is a contribution to gracious living, these places are filled with animation and enjoyment. Another survival from the Nordic past is that though Australia now produces wines of international quality, beer and rum remain the favorite national tipples.

Thus we may see that although Australia has long turned its back on Europe, the ghosts from its past still haunt it; and also that this vivid, life-embracing people seem to have imposed upon their instinct for enjoyment a spirit of naysaying self-denial.

RUSH-HOUR TRAFFIC congests the streets of downtown Sydney *(left)*. With more than two million people, Sydney is Australia's largest city. As more multistoried office buildings have gone up in the downtown area, the streets have become increasingly crowded in the morning and evening.

THRIVING PORT serving Sydney *(opposite)* is spanned by the famous steel Harbor Bridge, which here frames the moon in the early evening. About 4,000 ships a year dock at the wharves; Australia depends heavily on foreign trade for its present and future economic health.

Urban Growth Based on New Industries

Although the chief sources of Australia's wealth are still livestock and agriculture, the nation's primary hope for future prosperity and growth lies in industry. Every year 100,000 people arrive as immigrants; very few of these are needed on the farms and livestock stations, which are maintained by relatively few workers. Almost all the newcomers settle in the large cities along the coast, where the greatest concentration of the population resides. The Government strongly believes that if it cannot bring more people into the continent, it will be unable to resist the population pressure of overcrowded Asian countries. Heavy industry and immense public-works projects are helping to support these much-needed immigrants, while raising the standard of living for all.

COMMUTERS' FERRY conveys passengers *(left)* from Manly, one of Sydney's suburbs, to the heart of the city. Most suburbanites now prefer to drive to Sydney via the Harbor Bridge; but from Manly, which is on a peninsula, the most rapid way to commute is still the half-hour ferry trip.

A MINING TOWN provides full employment and a comfortable livelihood

A FAR-FLUNG COMPLEX of residential and industrial areas in Mount Isa, Queensland, is crowned by smoke rising from the copper smelter. Mount Isa Mines Limited, owned jointly by Australians and Americans, produces 70 per cent of the nation's copper, as well as silver, zinc and lead. The mines employ 4,000 workers, who live nearby in attractive homes.

LARGE ENTERPRISES employ thousands of workers and give the nation new industrial potential

ASSEMBLY LINE at the General Motors-Holden's factory 20 miles from Melbourne, owned jointly by the American automobile firm and Australians, turns out 245 Holden cars daily.

HUGE STRUCTURE, the Eucumbene Dam in New South Wales *(opposite)* is part of the Snowy Mountains Scheme, which will boost the nation's electricity and irrigate 1,000 square miles.

MASSIVE SHIPYARD at Whyalla in South Australia *(right)* is littered with gear as the 22,000-ton cargo ship *Musgrave Range* is constructed. The shipyard is the country's largest.

MORNING INFLUX of commuters hurries out of the Flinders Street railway station in downtown Melbourne. The second most populous city in Australia, Melbourne, with its growth rate of 50,000 people a year, may soon overtake its rival, Sydney. Melbourne is the capital of Victoria, which possesses 30 per cent of the nation's factories, employing 400,000 workers.

70

moments of recreation and socializing

SIDEWALK DRINKING outside the Canberra Bar in Sydney brings together a group of Sydneysiders from the cosmopolitan King's Cross district. Most of Sydney's bars close at 10 p.m.

LUNCH-HOUR BETTORS purchase lottery tickets at a state-run office in Sydney. The profits from Government lotteries help finance civic projects like the new Sydney Opera House.

NOONDAY BREAK is taken by office workers *(right)* in the small, tree-shaded Wynyard Park, one of the few green, peaceful enclaves in Sydney's noisy, crowded commercial district.

CHILD CARE within the kindergarten at the Scheyville Migrant Center near Sydney gives the children's parents time to search for jobs and homes. The center shelters new immigrants to Australia until the families are able to establish themselves.

RECENT ARRIVALS at the Migrant Center *(below)*, all of them Armenian, consult with Father William Vogt *(right)*, a priest and welfare officer. The center tries to place the newcomers and gives English classes to those who speak other tongues.

IMMIGRANTS, who form an ever larger part of the population, find a hospitable welcome

NATURALIZED CITIZEN Nick Tzanos, who came from Greece in 1955, packs peaches for sale to the local cannery. He is assisted by his wife and son; the family does almost all the work on their 20-acre property near Renmark, South Australia.

COPIOUS HARVEST of grapes is loaded by Nick Tzanos onto a tractor which his wife drives *(below)*. The child is their 20-month-old daughter. Nick owns the tractor and has paid back much of the $13,440 bank loan which he used to buy the land.

Schoolboys hurry to classes at Christ's College, a private secondary school in Christchurch, New Zealand. Founded in 1850, the school is

closely modeled on the great English public schools like Eton.

5

The Long White Cloud

AOTEAROA, or "long white cloud," is the name the Maoris gave to New Zealand when they discovered it, perhaps around 1,000 years ago. This poetic term, with its hint of seas, mountains and a fertile mystery, may seem a more fitting title for these lovely, lonely islands than the blunt Dutch of *Nieuw Zeeland;* and it may better serve to suggest in what ways this country differs so remarkably from the hot continental vastness of Australia. New Zealanders are often irritated, and understandably so, by being bracketed with Australia in the minds of other nations, as if the two countries and their peoples were identical, or New Zealand were even some sort of offshore island of the larger country. So one may perhaps best introduce New Zealand and its people by describing in what ways these nations are profoundly different.

To begin with, the two countries are 1,200 miles apart, or about the distance from Canada to Mexico. New Zealand, though 1,000 miles from north to south, and with 4,300 miles of coastline, is only 103,000 square miles in area, or about the size of the state of Colorado. Thus, from some peaks in the South Island, both coasts of the country can be seen, and there is nothing of the huge expanses of Australia. Yet within this much smaller area, there is, as we shall see, an infinitely greater scenic variety than is to be found in the larger country.

Although Australia has a long Pacific coast, being a continental country it looks inward and is not essentially a Pacific nation as New Zealand is. For New Zealand lies at the western base of the "Polynesian triangle," of which the apex is Hawaii and the eastern extremity Easter Island. New Zealand is thus committed to the Pacific, and in a real sense Auckland, the largest city of the North Island, is the number one city of Polynesia. This is all the more apparent when one considers the Maori presence in the country, in addition to which there are colonies of Samoans, Tongans and Cook Islanders, whose arrival in recent years constitutes a "second Polynesian invasion." And one is not surprised to find that Queen Salote of Tonga has a residence in Auckland as well as on the islands of which she is the monarch.

HISTORICALLY, the countries' origins are quite different, for as we have already seen, New Zealand was never a penal colony. Its people, from the outset, have been—except always for the Maoris—predominantly free and British. Even today New Zealand has not embarked on any massive crash program of immigration comparable to Australia's, but has confined itself chiefly to encouraging British migrants and those from northern Europe. This may be in part because the country knows that its small size and lack of industry prevent it from becoming a thickly populated nation. But it is also because New Zealanders adhere much more tenaciously to their "Britishness" than do Australians—though this is by no means to suggest that they wish to be anything other than themselves.

The chief economic difference is that whereas Australia has undergone, in the past two decades, what amounts to an industrial revolution, New Zealand's economy remains largely agricultural. More than 90 per cent of its exports are nonindustrial, and though only 16 per cent of the country's labor force is engaged directly in agriculture, its cities exist not so much for manufacture as to service this primary,

land-based production. It follows that while the Australian urban masses are, psychologically speaking, alienated from the land, no one in New Zealand is unaware of its vital importance to the country.

What effect do all these factors have on the New Zealand temperament? A New Zealander has said that "an Australian is an uninhibited New Zealander," and there seems some truth in this. The Kiwi character is certainly more subdued, less volatile, than the Australian, though none the less stalwart and reliable. The difference becomes striking when one encounters an Australian in New Zealand, for the Aussie has a bounce and buoyancy absent in the more composed and inward-looking Kiwi.

Between these two peoples, there is a curious kind of "nonlove affair." Australians, it is true, get on well with New Zealanders: they have fought together in two great wars, and they are politically allied in ANZUS and SEATO. It is also true that many Australians visit New Zealand—often girls on working holidays—and that there are thousands of Kiwis in Sydney alone, so that New Zealanders call it their "sixth city." On the other hand, one often meets New Zealanders who have traveled extensively in Europe, Asia and the United States but have never been to Australia at all, or only to change planes at its airports. A century ago New Zealand was for a time actually administered by New South Wales. But today, while there is a minority movement for the union of the two countries, this is not in the forefront of Australian or New Zealand political thinking. One might best describe the relationship as that of members of the same family who live in a similar region, respect each other with perfect cordiality, but have no particular desire to get together.

TO meet, the New Zealanders are not so ebullient as the Australians, but this can be an advantage in that they do not embarrass the visitor by an initial excess of cordiality. While hospitable and kindly (and remarkably honest), they can be obstinate and on occasion sultry, though this accompanies a certain diffidence not found in the brash Australians. On four subjects, New Zealanders can speak with absolute—and well-merited—authority: on how to fight, how to play games, how to make anything whatever on a do-it-yourself basis and how to grow farm produce of the highest quality. On other topics, however, they may often lapse into a noncommittal silence. Their speech is slower than that of the Australians, though delivered in a somewhat similar dry, sandy twang, and their language is even more laconic, an expression of high approval being simply "Good!" and fellow creatures described not as "mates" as in Australia but more anonymously as "jokers." A social advantage of a small country is that everyone seems to know where everyone else is located, and what he is currently doing—though from the point of view of developing individuality, let alone creative eccentricity, this close sense of community may have its disadvantages.

BETWEEN the two islands, North and South, there is a historic and still-present rivalry. The initial settlement was in the North, while later, in the 19th Century, the South Island grew to be the richer and more populous; but today, while the North Island is somewhat smaller, 70 per cent of the population lives in the warmer North, including most of the Maoris. The visitor to either island, if not prudent, may easily find himself involved in this traditional rivalry, so the best that he can do is describe these very different islands as objectively as possible, and hope to avoid the ire of either.

Of the South Island (which its inhabitants call "the Mainland"), one may immediately say that if its cities are the smaller, its scenic splendors are unquestionably more sensational. The fiords of the southwest, carved by ancient glaciers, pierce deep into the country's largest national park, which covers 3.3 million acres. Here are the island's largest lake—Te Anau, of 134 square miles—and one of the wonders of the world, the estuary of Milford Sound, whose sea canyon is flanked for 10 miles by mountains rising as high as 6,000 feet. Farther north, in the Southern Alps, is the country's highest peak, Mount Cook, called Aorangi—the "cloud piercer" —by the Maoris, which soars above 12,000 feet; and from the surrounding ranges, there descend great glaciers, like Franz Josef, eight miles long, which falls from 8,000 feet to a mere 700 feet above sea level. From Westland comes the jade that was so prized by the Maoris and is still dug for ornaments, among which the most nationally celebrated

—if not the most inviting—is the *tiki*, a grotesque, gnomelike figure said to be a symbol of fertility.

The older of the two large southern cities is Dunedin, which was founded in 1848 by Free Kirk Scotsmen, who gave it the Celtic name for Edinburgh. Set in the long inlet of Otago Harbor, it is a handsome place built largely of stone, which is unusual, since many constructions in the country, even important ones, are still made of wood. Once the chief commercial city of the nation, and the jumping-off point of a gold rush in 1861, Dunedin is now the center of the extensive sheep farming of Otago Province, which is the country's fifth-largest sheep producer. When Dunedin had a mere 13,000 people (it now has more than 100,000), its city fathers, like good Scots, founded, in 1869, the country's first university, that of Otago; and the surviving Caledonian instinct shows itself in ice curling in winter, Scottish bonnets on hard, shrewd heads, and a statue to Robert Burns in the city's center.

THE premier city of the South Island is Christchurch, with 233,000 people, well known to American naval airmen because its Harewood Airport has been the staging base for the U.S. Navy's Operation Deep Freeze in the Antarctic. Built on the banks of the river Avon, and adorned with innumerable public and private gardens, Christchurch is aptly called "the garden city of New Zealand"— though the visitor may sometimes feel that this profusion of well-ordered horticulture is perhaps excessively ornate, not to say competitive. For prizes are awarded by the municipality to the most burgeoning suburban streets, and extravagant herbaceous borders even extend up the concrete driveways to the residents' garages. Unlike most New Zealand cities, which have mountainous settings, Christchurch lies on the verge of the rich Canterbury Plains, of whose lamb, wool and grain production it is the commercial center. This means that the city is laid out on a spacious gridiron plan, though its harbor, Lyttleton, is reached through railroad tunnels under the rolling Port Hills. It was across these ranges that the first Anglican settlers came to found this extremely Church of England city.

If we cross narrow Cook Strait, which divides the islands, we at once reach the capital of the country,

Wellington, situated on the southwest tip of the North Island, on the splendid harbor of Port Nicholson. With its suburbs, it holds 256,000 people, but the steep hills rising all around the city curtail its expansion, and powerfully develop its citizens' thighs because so many houses must be reached by abrupt paths and laborious concrete stairways. Many of the buildings, even those of public note, are made of wood; and though Wellingtonians seem to be rather ashamed of these, and hasten to supplant them by concrete edifices, these buildings have enormous charm and greatly contribute to the style and simple dignity of this graceful capital city.

THOUGH not so dramatic as the South Island, the North can offer a far greater variety of scenic beauty. To the east, in the province of Taranaki, there rises "New Zealand's Mount Fujiyama," the perfect, isolated cone of Mount Egmont, an extinct volcano 8,260 feet in height. In the center of the island is Tongariro National Park, where there are still mildly active volcanoes, of which the greatest is Ruapehu, whose 9,175 feet make it the North Island's highest mountain. One of the most fertile regions is to the east, around Hawke Bay, where many of the country's remarkable wines are produced from 150 cellars that yield one million gallons every year. It is sad that New Zealanders, whose superb white wines have won praises from the renowned French gastronome André Simon, should prefer the inferior sweetened and fortified reds, the more so as the visitor may discover, near to Napier on Hawke Bay, a monastery of French brothers who have been producing fine wines since the 19th Century, which won international prizes as early as 1889.

In the northeast corner of the island, called East Cape, is some of the least known yet most glorious scenery of the country. For in the Raukumara Range, overlooking the Bay of Plenty, there are panoramas of a wild and dazzling grandeur; while in the subtropical foothills, there may be found great forests of the pungo, or giant tree fern, which is one of the nation's emblems, and vivid explosions of the crimson pohutukawa tree. But traveling westward, we shall enter a region that is renowned throughout New Zealand and indeed the world: the thermal areas around Wairakei and Lake Rotorua.

The town of Rotorua has some 21,000 inhabitants, but receives at least a quarter of a million visitors annually, of whom about a third come from overseas. A thousand wells bubble and spurt around the city, many of them gushing up in residential back yards and public parks, so that the town is overhung with clouds of sulphurous steam. It is also, to be entirely frank, saturated with a most unpleasant odor, but residents say they get used to this, and invalids welcome the curative qualities of the city's thermal baths. The show place of the area is the nearby Maori village of Whakarewarewa, home of the Arawa tribe, in whose extensive grounds there are caldrons, blowholes and geysers set in silica terraces from which steam and mud gurgle and splutter amid the clickings of a thousand cameras. The Maori village and its old fortress, or *pa*, are, truth to tell, somewhat squalid and disappointing, and with a fantastic site like this, one feels the New Zealanders could do rather better for the eager tourists. However, the resourceful Kiwis have elsewhere harnessed the sulphur springs to generate electricity; and to the south of Rotorua they have planted one of the largest man-made forests in the world, Kaingaroa, covering 284,000 hilly acres.

PAUSING to cast an amazed glance at the celebrated Waitomo Caves, which are hung with myriads of multicolored glowworms, we reach the largest city, port and industrial center of both islands, Auckland, with a population of 448,000, of whom thousands are urban Maoris. Auckland was once the nation's capital, and although it lost this honor to Wellington in 1865, it remains the most animated city of the country. Thanks to its superb, almost island setting between the two harbors of Waitemata and Manukau, and to the Aucklanders' passion for broad streets and lavish gardens, its enormous area has a density of only 5,000 people to the square mile (New York's is 22,000). Its climate is subtropical, and volcanic cones and islands rise around and even in it—the 644 feet of the extinct Mount Eden jut right up in the center of the town.

From Auckland, a long, narrow peninsula extends northwestward to the extremity of Cape Reinga, where the Pacific meets the Tasman Sea. From this point, where a sacred pohutukawa tree stands like a forlorn sentinel on the island's farthest rock, the souls of all faithful Maoris depart to the paradise of their mythical homeland of Hawaiki. On the west coast is the 90-mile beach where New Zealand's greatest gastronomic delicacy, the toheroa shellfish, may be gathered from the sands. On the east shore, there is the Bay of Islands, site of the first European settlement, and of the signature of the Treaty of Waitangi with the Maoris, a document whose tattered remnants may still be seen.

But all these areas of scenic splendor should not disguise the underlying fact that, in terms of economics, New Zealand is a vast agricultural factory and abattoir for the raising, slaughter and sale of millions of animals. One third of the country is devoted to pasture and to crops, and another third to marginal grazing and planted forests; the rest is mountainous country whose countless lakes and fast, steep rivers supply the nation's hydroelectric power. The islands hold 48 million sheep, six million cattle and two million dairy cows, and these account for New Zealand's being one of the world's largest exporters of meat and dairy produce and the second-largest exporter of wool, and for its selling abroad more lamb and mutton than all the other countries of the world combined. Every year some 7.5 million sheep, 18 million lambs, and close on a million each of cattle and calves are slaughtered and processed in 37 freezing works, while 321 dairy factories account for the nation's huge exports of butter and cheese. There are 77,000 farms of more than 10 acres, of which 27,600 are devoted to sheep, the highlands being mostly used for growing wool and the lower lands for breeding lambs. Dairy farming is next in importance, with intense cultivation in units averaging 50 to 100 acres with some 40 cows each. Production of beef is really secondary to sheep rearing, while crops are grown chiefly for local fodder, though grasses and clovers are exported.

This amazing achievement is due to a combination of rich natural resources and the intense use of scientific techniques. The country enjoys a mild, equable climate and a well-distributed rainfall, so that stock can graze outdoors throughout the year. But the early settlers, by clearing forest lands recklessly, eroded vast areas, and during the past 50 years the farmers and agriculturalists have had to restore the country from the subsoil up. There is thus an extremely close contact between agriculture and applied science, assured, for crops, by the Department of Scientific and Industrial Research and, for animals, by the Department of Agriculture. Together the two departments operate some 30 laboratories and experimental farms. In addition, there are numerous local "research associations" of farmers and agronomists, financed half by the landowners and half by governmental subsidy. The chief functions of these are the development of grassland pasture, artificial fertilization and farm mechanization.

One characteristic technique is the reclamation by the massive injection of cobalt and phosphates of one half of the three million acres of "black country" composed of volcanic pumice land. Another is the extensive use of "aerial top-dressing," by which aircraft are used for seeding, fertilization, and the spreading of insecticides, animal poisons and weed killers; planes are also used for mustering sheep and dropping fences. Since three fourths of the country is 650 feet or more above sea level, this technique is specially valuable in the many hilly regions. The waters from the heights are also used to generate electricity; and though the rivers are short, their descent to the sea is so rapid

PIONEERING THE WELFARE STATE

The remarkable system of laws which have made New Zealand a world leader in social-welfare legislation was begun in the 1890s. During that decade the New Zealand Parliament passed an extensive series of labor-relations acts which protected workers and their unions and set up machinery to establish minimum wages. It subdivided large estates, provided financial aid for small farmers and passed the Old-age Pensions Act—the first law of its kind in the English-speaking world. The Government also initiated bold schemes of public works. A second great period of social-welfare legislation began in 1936, when the Government fixed basic wages and decreed a 40-hour week for industry. In 1938 the Social Security Act was passed, which consolidated pension measures and also initiated New Zealand's present extensive health and medical benefit plans. Further laws passed since have enlarged the Government's participation in all of these areas until the state has become a foster father to all the nation's people and a partner of many of its farmers and businessmen.

that the country's largest, the 270-mile Waikato in the North Island, supplies 46 per cent of the nation's hydroelectric power. When the two islands are linked in 1965 by a 25-mile cable carrying power under Cook Strait, New Zealand will be able to assure the electrification of 98 per cent of all its homes, farms, factories and offices, one of the highest proportions in the world.

In nonagricultural raw materials the country is relatively poor, though there are coal and iron deposits and some petroleum and natural gas. Industrial production, though it employs 25 per cent of the labor force and accounts for a quarter of the gross national product, is chiefly for home consumption. As in Australia, a fifth of the workers are in Government service. The nation has as yet no heavy industry, though, as has been suggested, its real "heavy industry" is the massive production of wool, meat and butter.

Social security "from the cradle to the grave" is assured by New Zealand's governmental agencies. Education is free in state schools until the age of 19, though private denominational and independent colleges also exist. There are 18,000 students at the four universities and two agricultural colleges (including a number of Asians admitted each year under the Colombo Plan), and many of these are educated by Government grants. Old-age pensions, which New Zealand pioneered in 1898, are paid from the age of 60; there are family allowances for each child up to the age of 16, and the unemployed receive a weekly benefit. Under the Health Service, which costs $150 million annually, there is a weekly cash payment for the family of any breadwinner who is sick, all hospital costs are free, and part of a private doctor's fee is paid by the state.

THESE social services are financed by a levy on all wages, plus Government subsidies from general taxation. But though so cosseted by the state, New Zealanders hold an average of $5,340 of private life insurance and have bought two thirds of their own homes—though the Government, stepping in once again, encourages home purchase by permitting family allowances to be prepaid in a lump sum. To possess his own house—and a summer "bach" by the seaside—is every New Zealander's ambition.

With heavy taxation and extended social services, there is a considerable equality of real income, so that New Zealand is a country almost without very rich or poor. This may account for the country's characteristic social stability, as may also its predominantly Protestant culture, for the Roman Catholic community amounts here only to 14 per cent, while other minority sects—like that of the Mormon Church, whose young American apostles win many converts among the Maoris—do not greatly disturb the country's religious homogeneity. The abstemiousness of the people may be another factor, for the hotel bars close inexorably at 6 p.m., and the connoisseur of night life has to search very hard for it and confine himself almost exclusively to cosmopolitan Auckland and the capital, Wellington.

DOES this omnipresence of the state and the rigorous practical equality depress some of the nation's livelier spirits? It would seem that it does, for even more than in Australia an "immigration in reverse" accompanies New Zealand's efforts to increase its population. The most serious aspect of this trend is that the best-trained brains of the country often emigrate. Of these the chief precursor was Ernest Rutherford, who, at the universities of three continents, studied the composition of the nuclei of the atom, and first "split" it in 1921 at the Cavendish Laboratory in Cambridge, England. New Zealand's most illustrious son, on whom the Nobel Prize, more than a dozen foreign doctorates and an English barony were bestowed, Rutherford set a precedent of achievement overseas that many gifted young New Zealanders have since followed.

Then does this mean the islands are a fertile Eden from which its citizens are anxious to take flight? It is difficult to meet New Zealanders and believe so. With their short history, geographical isolation and intense struggle for material existence, they have had to put first things first and concentrate on material well-being. That this has resulted in a certain monotony in the social climate is not denied even by New Zealanders. But what is also certain is that in these radiant distant islands they have achieved to a high degree the fulfillment of the Good Fairy's three wishes to any favored child—the achievement of health, wealth and happiness.

Graders sample batches of rindless Cheddar cheese in a clinically clean butter and cheese factory located in Auckland, New Zealand.

The Merits and Limitations of an Ideal Society

For the average man, New Zealand is a utopia. In all areas of life, the Kiwis have made sensible and humane decisions. The cities are handsome and well planned; the predominantly agricultural economy is organized along scientific lines; Government welfare follows the individual from the cradle to the grave; and the whites and Maoris mingle freely and peacefully. If the exceptional New Zealander finds such a way of life unchallenging, nevertheless the typical wage earner considers the nation a haven from distress.

81

CLEANING THE POOL, Keith McKenzie, who owns the Milford Travel Lodge near Auckland, scours the bottom with a vacuum cleaner. A builder, he constructed the motel himself.

ADDRESSING CLUB MEMBERS, McKenzie speaks at a luncheon *(below)* held by the Takapuna Rotary Club. McKenzie is also an important member of the local chamber of commerce.

A SMALL BUSINESSMAN divides his time between work, community responsibilities and recreation

RIDING HER HORSE, 14-year-old Susan McKenzie *(right)* follows a dirt trail with her friend Carol Ripley. The McKenzies spend a large part of their income on outdoor recreation.

TAKING A SPIN, the McKenzie family skim the waves *(left)* in their powerboat. Next to McKenzie are his wife Dorothy and their son Craig. Behind them is their daughter Susan.

A FRIENDLY INTIMACY marks the nation's leading cities, which are clean, open and uncrowded

WELLINGTON, the national capital, glistens beside its deep harbor, which handles more tonnage than any other New Zealand port. Wellington is named after Britain's "Iron Duke."

CHRISTCHURCH prides itself on its Anglican Cathedral *(left)*, which dominates the city. The statue honors John Robert Godley, who brought Anglican pilgrims from England in 1850.

TIMBER HOUSES cling to a hillside *(opposite)* overlooking Wellington. New Zealand has many wooden buildings because timber is plentiful and withstands the frequent earth tremors.

*CALM SETTING marks
a farm region noted
for both its rich,
carefully cultivated soil
and its spectacular beauty*

SHROUDED MAJESTY of a huge volcano, Mount Egmont, looms above the Taranaki district on New Zealand's North Island. The farmland, which extends right up to the base of the mountain, is blessed with very rich soil. Early settlers burned off the trees, sowed the ground with grass, planted hedges to deflect strong winds and further enriched the soil with fertilizers.

RISING STEAM drifts in thick clouds over the geothermal-electric project at Wairakei, in the North Island's volcanic belt. Wells are drilled 2,000 feet or more below the surface of the ground to release steam and hot water from fissures in a layer of hot volcanic rock. Pipes conduct the steam to two Government-operated plants nearby which convert its energy into electricity.

*SCIENTIFIC METHODS are used
to harness steam power and to protect
and increase natural resources*

GOVERNMENT NURSERY at the New Zealand Forest Research Institute employs workers to graft buds onto pine seedlings in an effort to improve the trees before transplanting.

FORESTRY EXPERTS climb a numbered Radiata pine *(left)* to find buds for grafting. The forest is owned by New Zealand Forest Products, the nation's largest private forestry company.

The dominant force in Australian politics, Prime Minister Sir Robert Menzies (center, background) confers with premiers from the states

on a national roads policy at Parliament House in Canberra.

6

Stable Rule and Growing Wealth

AUSTRALIA and New Zealand are capitalist democracies, but with a difference. In political terms, there is a high degree of state intervention in everyday affairs, and the influence of labor and of trade unions is far greater than elsewhere. In the economic field, there are no large internal markets, so that both countries must exist by foreign trade, while at the same time each nation largely depends for its development on capital invested from overseas. To see how these factors operate in practice, let us examine the politics, and then the economies, of both countries.

Despite their British origins, the Australians in 1901 drew up a constitution more akin to that of the United States than that of Great Britain. The federal Government has "exclusive" powers—for example, those of defense, customs and external tariffs—and "concurrent" powers which it shares with the governments of the six states, but in case of dispute the federal law prevails. The federal High Court, like the American Supreme Court, is the final arbiter in the disputes, though a curious survival of British rule is that an appeal may still be made to the Privy Council of the United Kingdom, far off in London. In addition, the states have governors and the federation a Governor-General, but these men are not elected; they are appointed by the Queen—in her capacity not as Queen of England but of Australia—on the advice of the elected governments.

ELECTIONS to the federal and state Parliaments have two peculiarities. Voting is compulsory —and the penalty for not doing so is a $4.50 fine. It is also (except in Queensland) "proportional," meaning that the voters must state their order of preference for all candidates. At the first count of the votes, the "preferential" votes of the candidate receiving the least votes of all are distributed among his rivals, and so on until one candidate survives with a majority of both primary and preferential votes. This means that a man may win the most votes at the initial count and still be defeated—and also, as we shall see, that these preferential votes often influence the result of an election.

There are three chief parties operating both federally and in the states. The Liberal Party, which represents the conservative elements and the urban middle class, is usually allied with the smaller Country Party, which upholds the rural interests, and these at present rule together in the federal Parliament and in all states except two. The most formidable figure in Australian politics in recent years has been the Liberal Party leader, who was federal Prime Minister from 1939 to 1941, then took office again in 1949 and has remained there ever since: Sir Robert Gordon Menzies, a lawyer from Victoria, who was born in 1894 and who has been in politics since 1928. Brave in adversity, intolerant in power, he is ruthless, shrewd and marvelously sarcastic, and is a superb tactical empiricist. He is perhaps the only politician Australians either admire or fear.

The Australian Labour Party (called the ALP) holds power in Tasmania and New South Wales and is the chief opposition party elsewhere. Representing the trade union and working-class interests, and heavily Roman Catholic, it governed Australia during most of World War II and was once the strongest party in the country. Its decline and present

confusion can only be understood if one looks at Australia's two minor parties, the Communist and the Democratic Labour Party (DLP), and also if one realizes the direct involvement of the trade unions in Australian politics.

The Australian Communist Party is now the only pro-Moscow, or "caviar," party of the Pacific area, though there is a rival pro-Peking, or "dim-sim" (a kind of Chinese dumpling), group. The party has no parliamentary influence but is powerful in some trade unions, especially in the key industries and transport. Now, the trade unions are affiliated with the Labour Party, sometimes supplying as many as three quarters of the delegates to the ALP's state conferences. These, in turn, elect delegates to the party's federal conference, so that in the last resort the composition of the federal and state executive bodies, which determine Labour Party policy, depends on whoever controls the trade unions at the state level. In the late 1940s the unions under Communist control organized widespread political strikes, gained partial control of the Australian Council of Trade Unions and, through this, sought to dominate the Labour Party.

THE counterattack came from two sources. The first was unsuccessful, for although the Government had passed a Communist Party Dissolution Bill in 1950, the Australian High Court in 1951 declared that the bill was unconstitutional; and when the Labour Party leader, Dr. Herbert V. Evatt, insisted that the Communists should not be suppressed, Sir Robert Menzies held a national referendum by which a narrow majority of the voters upheld Dr. Evatt. But more effectively, opposition to the Communists was simultaneously being organized inside the unions themselves. Starting in 1946, the Labour Party built up "industrial groups" within the unions to combat Communist control; at the same time, Roman Catholic activists, sponsored by Bartholomew Santamaria and the Catholic hierarchy, launched a program called "The Movement," which recovered control of many of the unions. Mr. Santamaria, a man who even his many enemies admit possesses a great intelligence and a world view of politics unusual in Australia, remains a controversial figure, since his intervention has aroused the animosity not only of the Communist Party but of a large segment of the ALP, of many anti-Catholic Protestants and even of the more conservative members of the Roman Catholic community.

The eventual result of all this maneuvering was a fatal split in the ALP. For in the mid-1950s, Dr. Evatt, who by that time had been defeated in two general elections, found his party pulled one way by the Communists and the other by Santamaria's Roman Catholic "Movement." His handling of the Petrov Affair of Russian espionage had further alienated the party's right wing, and he was forced to make common cause with the Labour leftists, thereby enabling Communist influence to grow again within the unions. And so the Labour Party broke in two, with Santamaria's group becoming the new Democratic Labour Party and Dr. Evatt going into political oblivion. The DLP, though it has not won more than 10 per cent of any national vote, can determine ALP success because the preferential votes of DLP supporters are usually given not to the ALP but to the ALP's enemies, the Liberals. Thus it is that the three parties prominent in the federal and the state Parliaments—the Liberal, Country and Labour Parties—find themselves unduly influenced by the maneuvers of two much smaller groups, the minority Communist Party and its Roman Catholic rival, the DLP.

THIS does, however, provide the Liberal Party with a tremendous tactical advantage. Cohesive itself, except for a few mavericks, it has been able to declare to the electorate that the ALP is not only fatally divided but controlled by the 36 "faceless men" of its federal conference. Now while it is mere propaganda to say that these men, whom everybody knows, are "faceless," it is true that the ALP conference does decide parliamentary policy, rather than the caucus of the party's actual members of Parliament. A claim can thus be made that the Labour system is undemocratic, since its parliamentarians are responsible not to their electors but to an executive group of the Labour conference—which is elected largely by the trade unions.

Before the decline of the ALP, powerful Labour Prime Ministers, like Curtin and Chifley during and after World War II, had enough prestige to overawe the "faceless men" of the period. But Dr. Evatt's actions dissipated this power. At present, the members of the ALP's federal conference are divided about evenly between right and left, and the Liberals are extremely adroit at playing off one faction against the other. In addition, since Australians are more and more becoming property owners, the old dynamic of the Labour Party is decreasing, while the "welfare capitalism" of the Liberals makes a growing appeal.

STATE politics, with the years, have become increasingly less significant than federal, the more so as the great bulk of taxation is imposed by the central Government, which thereupon passes part of the revenue back to the states. Although the states complain about this, they show few positive signs of wanting to recover more of the unpopular right to tax; and this also means that, since they are largely dependent on federal grants, their attitudes toward the electorate tend to be less responsible. Nevertheless, their chief concern is for such matters as education, transportation and health, and also for housing, for which they may get federal loans. Australia spends some $600 million annually for social-service payments for pensions, maternity and child endowments, and sickness and unemployment benefits, while almost $200 million annually goes to the Health Service.

By comparison with Australian politics, those in New Zealand seem of crystalline simplicity. Since the provincial governments were abolished in 1876, and the upper Federal House in 1951, there is only one Parliament for the whole country. It has 80 seats, of which four are reserved for Maoris—Maori electors vote for these four on a special Maori roll. There are five parties: the National, which came into power in 1960; Labour, which had its heroic days in the pre- and post-World War II years, but which is now in opposition; the Social Credit Party, which represents disaffected small rural and urban interests—or rather, fails to represent them, since it has no parliamentary members; the Liberal Party, a rightish group also without electoral support; and the Communist Party, which, as in Australia, has had influence in the trade unions but not in Parliament, and which, unlike the Australian party, is Peking-inclined rather than Muscovite. The Prime Minister since 1960 has been Keith Jacka Holyoake, a farmer born in 1904, who had been Minister of Agriculture for eight years before leading the National Party.

In general terms, the National Party has the support of the farming, industrial and prosperous urban groups, but since there is often a conflict of interest between agriculture and industry, many manufacturers give their support to Labour. Despite the overthrow of Labour power in 1960, the state under the Nationals still controls the economy to a great extent. The Reserve Bank is state-owned, as is the Bank of New Zealand, which finances a third of the country's trade. The state also intervenes in insurance and transport; it owns most of the installations that produce electric power and many of those producing coal; and it owns four fifths of the forest industries and actively finances home building. Governmental control of marketing, imports and price levels has also been maintained, since state regulations to cushion slumps and inflation are deemed indispensable by all the political parties.

It will be seen that the field of political maneuvering is much more restricted in New Zealand than in Australia, and that the two chief parties, National and Labour, are far closer together than their Australian counterparts. Thus Arnold Nordmeyer, the Labour opposition leader, is not trade union oriented like Arthur Calwell of Australia, but is a middle-class intellectual more like many Labour leaders in Britain. The swing to the Nationals, and the emergence of splinter groups like the Liberals and Social Credit, may indicate some measure of public revolt against the paternalism of the New Zealand Government— as may also the state's yielding to demands for an Ombudsman, the only such functionary to be found outside Scandinavia. The Ombudsman's duty is to act as watchdog for the public against governmental

bureaucracy, and to investigate complaints against the excessive use of state authority.

As in Australia, the trade unions intervene actively in Labour politics, and have the further advantage that a Labour act of 1936 made membership in them compulsory. While this measure has naturally increased trade union power, it has also had the effect of diluting the unions' militancy and of encouraging the creation of rival employers' federations. Under the Arbitration Act of 1954, both strikes and lockouts are prohibited; trade disputes are referred to Conciliation Councils and, if necessary, to Arbitration Courts, whose findings have the force of law. Australia has a similar law whereby wages, hours and working conditions are regulated by industrial tribunals, but owing to the greater militancy of Australian workers and trade union officials, industrial disputes are more frequent than in New Zealand.

To defend these political institutions and each country's prosperity, it must in truth be said that Australia and New Zealand rely far more on foreign treaties than on their own endeavors. In 1962-1963, Australia spent less than 3 per cent of its gross national product on defense, and its armed forces are modest. There is no conscription, and though rates of pay are high, voluntary enlistment is not enthusiastic. Apart from the reserve Citizen Forces, the regular manpower of Australia's three armed services numbers only 50,000, and much of their equipment is obsolete or inadequate, though efforts have been made to remedy this, particularly in regard to aircraft. New Zealand, which now spends around $73 million annually on defense, has only 12,000 regular servicemen under arms.

To any suggestion that their defense effort is inadequate, Australians and New Zealanders, while largely agreeing, will also reply that their first essential task is to create bastions of economic wealth

A NATION WITH NO CONSTITUTION

Like the England which once ruled it, New Zealand is democratically governed by a Parliament made up of elected representatives of the people, but has no constitution. Again like Great Britain, New Zealand is guided by a handful of laws and acts passed by Parliament itself—and by a body of long-standing conventions. When Great Britain granted independent government to New Zealand in 1852, it established an act for the country which in many ways functioned like a constitution. However, in one important respect the act is not a true constitution: most of its clauses can be amended or repealed by Parliament through the normal legislative procedure. The Electoral Act of 1956, covering issues such as the franchise, balloting and apportionment of electoral districts, serves in part as a constitution, but it may also be amended or discarded by Parliament.

and power in the Southwest Pacific. Judged from this point of view, their achievement is undeniably impressive. Industrial expansion in both countries has proceeded at a fantastic rate, but since, as we have seen, New Zealand is chiefly a nonindustrial producer, while even in industrialized Australia four fifths of all exports are still agricultural, the rural production of the two countries should first be described.

This involves some rather staggering statistics. Australian rural holdings cover more than a billion acres, on which there wander 158 million sheep, 13 million beef cattle and five million dairy cows, while on 15 million acres wheat is grown, the chief of the country's many crops. The gross value of all rural production is three billion dollars, of which more than two thirds is exported. Surprisingly, this enormous effort is achieved by only 11 per cent of the national labor force. Attempts are still being made, under a long-standing "closer settlement" scheme, to encourage the extension of small farms through state subsidy, particularly to ex-soldiers; on a larger scale, meanwhile, professional investors are increasingly moving into the pastoral industries. In New Zealand, the rural production (see Chapter 5) has a gross value of about one fourth that of Australia.

INDUSTRIAL production in both countries was greatly accelerated by World War II, but especially in Australia. Manufacturing and commerce now account for 45 per cent of Australia's work force and more than one third of the gross national product, and 59,000 factories produce goods of an annual net value of $5.3 billion. Being rich in iron ore, coal, and almost every mineral, and with petroleum and natural gas having at last been discovered, Australia has now built up a heavy industry of mining, engineering, shipbuilding, chemicals, automobiles and oil refining which is capable of producing all kinds of goods except at the most sophisticated technical levels. Protected by tariffs, this industry can supply most of the domestic market, but since this is small, a great export effort has been necessary.

A big problem has been that of capital. Australia has a strong banking structure, headed by the Commonwealth Bank and its subsidiaries and supported by numerous trading banks, and so internal savings are able to supply much of the needed funds, and

the federal and state Governments earmarked some $525 million for capital investment in a recent year. But the country still greatly relies on funds from overseas, and the total foreign stake in Australia now amounts to several billion dollars, most of it from Britain, the United States and Canada. As much as a quarter of Australian industry is overseas-owned and 40 per cent of it overseas-controlled, though the steel industry remains in Australian hands.

THIS reliance on foreign capital causes anxiety, comparable to that felt by Canada in relation to U.S. investment. Australia needs these funds to develop its industry—and it also needs to acquire managerial and industrial techniques from overseas firms. But the country's economists are concerned that the payment of overseas dividends eventually may reverse the favorable balance of payments that the initial overseas investment has engendered, and that payments to overseas shareholders may rise faster, proportionately, than the national income. They are also bothered by the fact that foreign investors are interested only in high-profit industries, and that American investors, in particular, are reluctant to back Australian companies that permit Australians to invest in them too, preferring to operate through subsidiaries. A minor, if important, transformation of Australian commerce will come in February 1966, when the coinage will be switched from English denominations to a decimal dollar currency. New Zealand will follow suit the year after.

In New Zealand, because of the relative scarcity of raw materials, the industrial effort is confined chiefly to engineering, light shipbuilding, electrical goods, paper and textiles. Almost enough oil for the country's needs is refined locally, and hydroelectric and geothermal (steam) power is actively exploited. One fifth of the gross national product is devoted to capital investment, though as in Australia, there are large foreign holdings, especially by British investors. Government policy toward overseas capital is to welcome these funds while trying to ensure that part of the equity capital of New Zealand firms should be held inside the country.

The use of scientific research to encourage production in all sectors is intense in both countries. The work of agricultural scientists in New Zealand has already been described (see Chapter 5), and in Australia the chief governmental organ is the CSIRO, or Commonwealth Scientific and Industrial Research Organization, whose work complements the research effort of the universities. The CSIRO has a staff of 5,000, many of whom come from overseas and 750 of whom are advanced scientists. It is organized into 33 agricultural, scientific and industrial divisions and its annual expenditure runs to some $36 million—though this is only a tiny percentage of the gross national product and considerably less proportionately than is spent for research in the U.S.

In a huge country like Australia, and even in mountainous 1,000-mile-long New Zealand, transportation is of key importance, and here the greatest change in the past two decades has been the extension of air transport. Australia has two main internal lines, TAA, which is Government-owned, and Ansett-ANA, which is a private company; New Zealand has only one major internal airline, NAC. Australia's overseas line is QANTAS, which in a sense is an extension of the Department of External Affairs, since its extreme efficiency makes the Australian "presence" known in every continent. It is one of the few international airlines to make a profit, which in 1962-1963 amounted to three million dollars. A large percentage of its passengers are non-Australians, and its success is due largely to the fact that it rejects purely "prestige" flights and, by following Australian trade patterns, operates only in areas where traffic to Australia can be assured. (It also prides itself on creating the only English word in which the letter "q" is not followed by a "u"; its name stands for Queensland and Northern Territory Aerial Services.) The New Zealand international airline is TEAL (for Tasman Empire Airways Limited), which fulfills, if less extensively, a

---

OFFICIAL AND UNOFFICIAL TERMS

Commonwealth of Australia: The official name of Australia, dating from the Federation of 1901.

The Federation: An unofficial but widely used term for Australia.

Commonwealth of Nations: The full name of the present-day alignment of those countries which until 1931 constituted the major segments of the British Empire, and which today are self-governing. Australia and New Zealand are both members. Commonwealth countries generally cooperate with each other in foreign affairs; they are tied to each other through a host of economic agreements; and most of them recognize the titular sovereignty of the British Crown.

The British Commonwealth: An unofficial but widely used term for the Commonwealth of Nations.

Great Britain: England, Scotland and Wales.

Britain: A familiar synonym for Great Britain.

The United Kingdom: Great Britain plus Northern Ireland.

---

similar function of national development and external propaganda.

External shipping, especially that of New Zealand, is still largely in British hands. But coastal shipping is mostly locally owned, and both countries have national shipping lines. Australian shipyards can now build vessels of more than 40,000 tons. Railroads are being extended, and the Australians, with 25,000 miles of track at present, have plans to overcome the difficulties caused by their three different gauges. All this production and equipment must serve, if both countries are to preserve their high living standards, to reach and enter markets overseas at competitive prices and to stand up to fierce and growing competition.

The chief Australian exports remain wool, wheat and cattle, and of total exports valued at around three billion dollars, the chief buyers are the United Kingdom, Japan and the United States, in that order. Japan is now Australia's largest wool buyer, replacing the U.K. For wheat, Communist China is the chief client, taking two million tons. Of the total beef export of 290,000 tons, three fourths goes to the U.S.—against intense opposition from American beef producers. This represents a big change from the trade patterns of the years before World War II, for Britain, which at that time took fully half of Australian exports, now buys only one fifth. Japan is replacing Britain as Australia's best potential customer, being interested especially in wool, wheat and copper. Total exports to Japan now run at almost $400 million annually, and since Australia takes only about $145 million in imports from Japan, there are Japanese complaints that this is a one-sided bargain; but to this the Australians reply that these figures should be judged in relation to the two populations, which govern the size of these markets. There can be no doubt that Australia, disillusioned by British efforts to enter the Common Market, will increasingly try to orient its trade toward Asia and the United States. It is this that explains the remarkable trade "love affair" between Australia and Japan, which would have seemed inconceivable a mere 20 years ago.

Another imbalance of trade that has political consequences is the relationship between Australia and New Zealand; for while Australia's exports to New Zealand—chiefly of wheat, sugar and industrial goods —were worth $140 million in 1962-1963, New Zealand sent only $40 million in export goods to Australia during the same period. This means that when there is talk of union with Australia, New Zealanders wonder whether, without import restrictions, their markets might not under those circumstances be even more flooded by Australian goods.

Exports of metals and manufactured articles, though they are increasing, are less remunerative to Australia so far, though iron ore and the country's exceptionally cheap steel find good markets. There is also a growing foreign sale of diesel engines, electronic goods and even motor vehicles. The chief imports to Australia come from Britain, the United States, Germany and Japan, and there is at present a favorable trade balance, while $1.8 billion in gold and foreign currencies has been accumulated.

WITH New Zealand, too, there is a reorientation of marketing, for while the United Kingdom remains the chief buyer, New Zealand is seeking new markets in Europe, the United States, Canada, Japan and the rest of the Pacific area, and even in Latin America. Thus, exports to the U.K. have fallen from almost three fourths of the total in 1948 to about half. The country's best customer after the U.K. is America, which takes about one seventh of New Zealand's exports. Out of total exports worth $900 million annually, pastoral produce accounts for more than 90 per cent, the chief items being wool, meat and dairy produce. A difficulty of all New Zealand export efforts is the immense distance of the country from all its markets, which adds at least 10 per cent in transport costs to the initial prices. But New Zealand Trade Commissioners and other officials in the chief receiving countries are very active; they have at present, for instance, embarked

on a campaign to try to persuade the Japanese to eat not only mutton but the more costly lamb as well.

Australia and New Zealand are not usually thought of as countries with a colonial question, and it comes as something of a surprise to find that both these young nations have been faced with problems of decolonization. The chief of these arises in the territories of Papua and New Guinea, where the United Nations has set Australia a triple task: of conducting a full economic survey and producing a development plan; of graduating at least 100 native students from Australian universities annually; and of establishing a 100-member parliament by 1964. The survey has been undertaken with the help of the World Bank, the educational effort is being intensified, and elections have already been held. The new legislature is not quite as large as that proposed by the U.N., but consists of 64 members, of whom 10 are officially appointed, while the rest, elected on a common roll, must include at least 10 Europeans. Two features of the 1964 election were that 16 Europeans were elected by indigenous voters and that several hundred people insisted on voting for Lyndon B. Johnson, despite Mr. Johnson's not having announced his candidacy in that contest.

New Zealand yielded to Western Samoa's demand for independence in 1962, making this the first fully independent nation of the Polynesian Pacific. But New Zealand still subsidizes Western Samoa to the extent of $467,000 annually and Samoans have unrestricted access to the New Zealand mainland. The 18,000 Cook Islanders are constitutionally citizens of New Zealand, though they have a local legislature and are moving toward self-government in association with their present colonial overlords.

ALL of this may seem surprising when one remembers the ambitious plans of some Australian and New Zealand politicians of the 19th Century to conquer vast areas of the Pacific, and also the armament both countries possessed at the height of World Wars I and II. But it must be said that both nations have exercised an unusual restraint in dealing with their weaker neighbors. Perhaps this is because, having so recently been colonies themselves, the Australians and New Zealanders have never been greatly enamored of colonialism.

Students from Massey University in New Zealand observe a herd of Jerseys during a field demonstration at the school's dairy farm.

Remarkable Achievements in the Public Interest

The Governments of Australia and New Zealand serve their citizens through a system of institutions which rank high by international standards. In addition, these services are admirably suited to the specific needs of the countries themselves. The schools in both nations, particularly the universities, maintain an excellence in scholarship; in New Zealand the welfare program is among the most comprehensive and advanced in the world, providing free medical attention for all and stipends for large families.

BOARDING STUDENTS say grace at the state-run Maitland Boys' High School in New South Wales, Australia. Like several other schools, Maitland operates a boarding hostel for students who live in rural areas so remote they cannot commute.

MILITARY CADETS at Maitland (*below*) learn to operate a Bren gun. The school corps, with 223 members, is the largest in the state outside Sydney; the boys join at 14. Such training is a prominent feature in Australian high schools.

*THE UNIVERSITY OF SYDNEY is
swamped by huge new enrollments
but keeps abreast of modern scholarship*

Students pass new buildings at the University of Sydney,

AT THE STUDENT UNION, male undergraduates eat
lunch outdoors *(left)*. The university's enrollment has
grown from 3,000 students in 1939 to about 15,000 now.

DURING FREE TIME, casually dressed students listen to recorded music by earphone in the new Fisher Library, which has won two awards for fine architecture.

IN CONSULTATION, an assistant *(left)* discusses the anatomy of a toad with a zoology student. Although classes are large, assistants give individual attention.

which is Australia's largest institute of higher education.

AT THE BLACKBOARD, Dr. Rex Meyer addresses a beginning zoology class *(right)*. Australia has 10 universities, all of them secular and operated by the state.

SOCIAL WELFARE *in New Zealand assures complete health care for everyone*

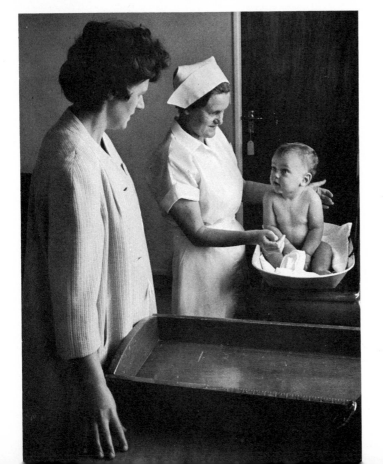

MOLDING CLAY, camp matron Marie Cameron instructs children at the Glenelg Health Camp *(above)* in Christchurch, New Zealand. There are nine state-subsidized health camps in the country, providing a wholesome atmosphere for underprivileged and emotionally disturbed children.

WEIGHING A BABY, Violet Walmsley, a nurse from New Zealand's Plunket Society, checks on an infant's health *(left)* as his mother watches. The society, a state-aided voluntary organization, provides instruction for mothers and operates six hospitals for babies who need special care.

ASSISTING PATIENTS, a student nurse at Wellington's Dominion School for Dental Nurses conducts two children *(opposite)* down an aisle between numbered chairs. Such nurses give children complete tooth care in the nearly 1,000 dental clinics in New Zealand's public schools.

A Maori addresses a war veterans' league in Whakarewarewa on the North Island of New Zealand. The meetinghouse is elaborately

decorated with figures of gods and heroes in ancient Maori style.

7

The
Native Sons

"THE inhabitants of this country are the miserablest people in the world." So wrote William Dampier of the Australian aborigines when he first saw them in 1688. Three centuries later we may ask if their condition is still the same.

The aborigines began to arrive in Australia about 25,000 B.C. or perhaps earlier, at a time when there were land bridges between the Australian continent and New Guinea and the Asian mainland to the north. They apparently came in three great migrations, and though their lands of origin are uncertain, they may be related to certain primitive tribes found in Ceylon, Malaya and Japan. Australia was more fertile then, with rivers and lakes that have since disappeared. But though the aborigines evolved a highly complex primitive culture, the return of the seas to the north cut them off for millennia from their original homelands and thus from their former civilizations. The Australian aborigines remained a nomadic hunting people, with no knowledge of seed-bearing plants and, except for the dingo, no domestic animals. Those who were spared European influence remain living fossils of Stone Age man.

There were perhaps 300,000 aborigines when the Europeans occupied Australia, and today there are some 40,000 purebloods and perhaps as many half-castes. They are mostly to be found in the northern regions of the country, and it is principally in the far north, in Arnhem Land and the adjacent islands, that the old ways of aboriginal life survive. Elsewhere, about one half of the detribalized aborigines live on some 40 Government and 60 "mission" stations which are rather like a cross between a rural village and a collective farm. These stations are conducted by 750 Government officers and 500 religious missionaries and are supported by Government grants of $12.2 million a year. The remainder of the detribalized aborigines work as foresters, as stockmen on the cattle stations, or in the rural townships as laborers on the railroads, in factories or in domestic service. Some 13,500 aboriginal children receive primary education, and 400 secondary. One surprise is the number of half-castes who have settled recently in the big cities; it is thought there are several thousand in Sydney alone. Another is that, thanks largely to medical care, the number of aborigines is at last increasing.

WHY had they so catastrophically declined? On the foundation of the colony, Governor Phillip was at first sympathetic to the aborigines, if only from motives of prudence. But when the European population grew, and the aborigines saw their best food-gathering areas taken and their sacred sanctuaries violated, they reacted aggressively, and by 1806 soldiers were driving them out of the colonized regions. Thereafter, though there was never anything like a large-scale "aboriginal war," these native Australians were pushed back into the interior or were exterminated. They were hunted like kangaroos, offered food filled with arsenic, introduced to liquor and encouraged to fight among themselves. Moreover, the undermining of their social structure and religious beliefs led to their moral and physical disintegration. The last male Tasmanian aborigine died in 1869, and by that time aborigines everywhere were on the decline and in retreat. It is not too much to say that Australians have solved their racial problem by virtually eliminating it.

Even today, except among artists and anthropologists, the public interest in the aborigines is superficial and sentimental. In addition to place names, some 150 aboriginal words have entered the Australian language, and the native boomerang (which few Australians know how to throw) has become a sort of national symbol. But in real terms, except in the regions of aboriginal settlement, Australians have simply banished this people from their consciousness. It is true that there is an Australian Institute of Aboriginal Studies, and in the universities there are chairs of aboriginal anthropology which afford extraordinary opportunities to scholars since new languages and tribes are being discovered even today. But this effort is concerned not so much with preservation as with recording the cultures of this people before it is too late. For most anthropologists agree that the ancient customs will probably have disappeared within 25 years.

The outlook for the Europeanized aborigine is less bleak, particularly in the rural areas. The huge, lonely cattle stations of the north and west have difficulty in recruiting white labor, particularly since the pay is poor by urban standards—$18 to $27 a week, with keep, being usual. Aboriginal stockmen will work for as little as nine dollars weekly, and therefore they outnumber whites on many cattle stations. Owners assert, however, that this is not as cheap as it looks, since aborigines, though competent stockmen, are hard on the horses and do not work well without supervision. In addition, by the term "keep," they understand not just that of themselves and their families but of any blood relations who may drop in at the station on a "walkabout." The cattle owners declare that if they could get white labor they would do without the aborigines altogether. But this is unlikely, and it seems that the aborigines will play an increasing and vital part in the cattle industry.

ABORIGINES have the right to vote in the federal elections. However, those who live on governmental or mission stations, or on the tribal reserves, are deemed "wards of the state," and some are subject to certain restrictions, among them a prohibition against drinking liquor. But an aborigine may opt out of being a state ward, in which case he loses his right to the subsidized upkeep of the mission station and must fend thereafter for himself. Since half-castes are never wards of the state, there is thus the curious situation that two kinds of aborigines may drink and another not. The whole question seems somewhat academic, for while it is true that aborigines are very bad drinkers, they seem to have no difficulty in getting "grog" and carrying it off to the creek bed for a carousal.

Measures are being debated for the lifting of all restrictions on all aborigines and according them full equality of legal—if not economic—rights. Despite opposition from cattle owners and missionaries, it seems likely that this will come to pass. Even those who do not deem the aborigines worthy of this privilege support the change for two chief reasons. The first is that, given the international pressures against racialism, Australians feel they cannot appear to have any second-class citizens. The second arises from a genuine feeling that since this is a democracy, it must not be racially exclusive.

These measures, if enacted, together with the increasing aboriginal employment in agriculture and even small urban industry, make it probable that the importance of the mission stations will gradually decline. The choice between menial, if independent, employment outside them and the cushioned servitude within them must be a hard one for the aborigines. Yet despite the devotion of the Government servants and missionaries who conduct the stations, these places often seem depressing, and the aborigines who live on them look lackluster and resigned. Among urban aborigines, on the other hand, and among the mineworkers of the northwest, there are some signs of political militancy. With the gradual detribalization of primitive aboriginal life and the decline of the mission stations, it would thus seem likely that the aborigines will eventually become urban and rural workers like any others. If this does happen, white Australia will be faced with a color

BARK PAINTING made by an aborigine from northern Australia pictures kangaroos, lizards and emus. Such paintings are often done to ensure success in hunting.

problem—though on a minor scale—which has hitherto, because of the isolation of the aborigines, been only latent. Foreseeing this, some whites speak blandly of "breeding the aborigines out of existence," which is not inconceivable, since their numbers are so small. But opposing this concept are a growing pride in their ancestry among the aborigines and admiration of their culture among a small elite of the whites.

Among the few aborigines who have managed to break through into the white world, the artists, such as the late painter Albert Namatjira or the operatic tenor Harold Blair, have been the most successful, though aborigines have become soldiers, sportsmen and churchmen, too. But the chief admiration of white Australians is for aboriginal artists of the past and present who belong to the old tribal society, and particularly for their plastic arts. Most strange and beautiful are the Kimberley cave paintings of northwest Australia, which represent the mysterious Wondjinas, ancestral spirits of the distant "dream time" before the aboriginal world was created. Painted in vivid ochered colors, these gigantic, solemn figures gaze down timelessly, and still have the

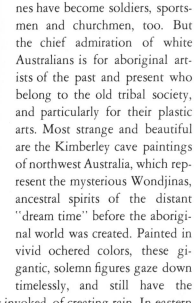

power, if suitably invoked, of creating rain. In eastern Australia are huge rock engravings depicting hunts and ceremonials in a realistic manner, laboriously punched into the sandstone with stone implements, since the aborigines knew no metals. Most impressive of all are the lofty grave posts of Bathurst and Melville Islands, great circular columns from which irregular shapes have been hollowed out, and whose surfaces are incised with vivid patterns.

These are still being made, as are the paintings on stringybark of birds, beasts and fish. The popularity of these arts among Europeans is unfortunately such that, spurred on by resourceful dealers, the aborigines are now producing inferior imitations. Another dying art is that of body painting for ceremonial occasions, in which the performers' naked bodies are decorated with colored designs of infinite variety, the paint in turn being covered with variegated downs of birds. An aboriginal "applied art" is that of their weapons of wood and bone, chiefly the spear and boomerang, whose shapes, though utilitarian, have an immense grace and vivacity. Of the boomerang, there are two types: the heavy hunting implement and the famous returning boomerang. This is really a toy which, when thrown, spins a circle 100 yards in diameter before falling, after several smaller circles, near the thrower's feet.

ABOUT aboriginal tribal life, there seems much that is attractive and much that is repellent or alarming. Except for simple household utensils, aborigines have no conception of private possessions, and lands are held collectively by the group or tribe. Hunting and fishing are collective enterprises, and the sharing of food with others is a prime obligation, while even wives—or one of them—may be offered to a kinsman. Fighting is only for vengeance or to punish violation of taboos, and is rarely on a tribal scale. Less attractive are certain elements of the aboriginal diet. The most various creatures are devoured, ranging from crocodiles and the 1,000-pound sea mammal, the dugong, to the fat, white witchetty grub which is dug out of the ground. Most remarkable of all are the aborigines' endurance and resource in snatching life from a hostile environment. They can track animals over great distances, make fire by rubbing sticks together and find water by draining moisture from tree roots.

Socially, aboriginal life is dominated by the male elders, who enforce, with relentless discipline, the worship of ancestors, complex totemic rules and the preservation of the sacred sites. It is they who organize the corroborees, or ceremonial tribal gatherings, and teach to the young the profusion of song cycles and dances by which deities are placated and tribal myths preserved. This involves prodigious feats of memory, for the aborigines have no writing, unless one admits that their variety of "message sticks" carved with symbols conveying information constitutes writing of a kind. Initiation is a painful process, especially for the boys, who are circumcised, often by subincision. The "magic men" have the power of pointing the "killer bone" at an offender,

who then believes that he must die. These sorcerers can conjure up malignant spirits like the Bunyip, a creature which has even entered into white Australian mythology. But a benevolent magician can brew love potions, an advantage for a people who, allowed by custom a certain amount of sexual license, lead quite active amorous lives.

It is thought that, when the Europeans came, there were perhaps 300 to 600 tribes in Australia. Although most tribes have shrunk and many have vanished, it is impossible not to be impressed by the aborigines' survival for thousands of years in a continent which even Europeans with modern technology still find, in so many areas, to be hostile to human habitation. In appearance the pureblood aborigines vary in color between red-brown and black, have dark, wavy hair and are usually bearded, and their deep-set brown eyes have a penetrating, melancholy gaze. Their limbs are long and slender and their step is light and swift. To the stranger—understandably—they are cautious and secretive, but on closer acquaintance they seem gentle, crafty and quick-spoken, although still withdrawn.

WITH the Maoris of New Zealand, we are in a different world. For the Maori (the word rhymes with "dowry") is a tough, able, handsome and resourceful figure, who strides through the streets of Auckland, or the bush tracks of the North Island, with a bold and confident demeanor. The Maoris know that, in the past, they have resisted the *pakeha,* or white New Zealander, have fought as valiantly as he in both World Wars, and can, for that matter, take him on at the national prestige game of Rugby football. Their people include scholars, professional men and eminent political leaders. Most vitally of all, the Maoris are still landowners: there is no question of their being banished to reserves and told they must not drink. Moreover, though they are a minority, their population is rapidly increasing, and 60 per cent of their people are under 21, compared with 40 per cent among other New Zealanders. The Maoris are further sustained by knowing that they form part of a gifted and tenacious Polynesian people spread all over the Pacific.

The white New Zealander must thus come to terms with the Maori, and broadly speaking, he has risen to the occasion. For there can be few countries in the world where harmony between races is so effective. There are irritants in the Maori-*pakeha* relationship, but there are no neuroses. The social relationships between the two peoples may not be intimate, but there is little overt hostility. For a *pakeha* to treat a Maori with contempt would be contrary to the public mood—apart from being highly dangerous.

LEGEND has it that the warrior Kupe, coming from the mythical Maori homeland of Hawaiki (which may have been Tahiti, or perhaps the Cook Islands), discovered the North Island round about 925 A.D., and returned to bring the good news to his people. According to some anthropologists, two other Polynesian peoples, the Morioi and the Moa Hunters, may have rediscovered the country before the Maoris finally returned. This is uncertain, but Maori legend and modern research agree that at a date somewhere near 1350 a considerable group of Maoris in a fleet of canoes, carrying stores and navigating by the stars (or else drifting accidentally), sailed 2,000 miles across the Pacific to settle their new island home.

Maori society, at this early date, was already highly evolved, and consisted of chieftains, commoners and slaves. But despite these divisions, social life was communal rather than individualistic—as indeed Maori life has remained. The great pleasures of the people were debate and warfare, for the Maoris were, and are, a highly eloquent and belligerent people. As they had no written language, they developed to an extraordinary degree their powers of memory, so that even today Maori elders can recite interminable tribal genealogies. They were also cannibals, and though apologists maintain that this cannibalism was strictly a ritual and almost a "religious" custom, it seems unlikely; and at all events, contemporary Maoris are not ashamed of this practice in their recent past. A sardonic Maori wit, discussing racial relations, remarked recently to a visitor that his people "had digested the European problem."

By the time of the arrival of Captain Cook, in 1769, there were perhaps 200,000 Maoris on the islands, mostly on the North Island. As has already been related in Chapter 2, the Maori interests were not protected, and as a consequence of their war with the whites, the loss of their land and the introduction of European diseases, the Maori population had by 1896 shrunk to 42,000, and they were thought to be a dying people. The revival began in the 1890s with the foundation of the Young Maori Party by three brilliant young men, all of whom subsequently sat in the New Zealand Parliament and were knighted, and of whom the most illustrious was Te Rangi Hiroa, or Sir Peter Buck, who later became a professor of anthropology at Yale University and director of Honolulu's Bishop Museum, which specializes in Polynesian studies. The Maoris eventually developed resistance to European ailments, medical care improved, and most vitally of all, the loss of land was checked, if not halted, so that today they own four million acres, of which two and a half million are developed.

TODAY the Maoris number 180,000, or 7 per cent of New Zealand's population, and their birth rate reached 38 per 1,000 in 1961, one of the highest in the world. Family allowances from the Government (Maori wits call it "stallion money") help to account for this, as does the more important fact that in the close-knit Maori society no orphaned child, or even an illegitimate one, would conceivably be without an eager foster parent. There is a Minister of Maori Affairs, with an energetic department staffed partly by Maoris. An official Maori Education Foundation encourages and subsidizes secondary and university education; and there is a Maori Council of tribal executives, an advisory body elected by the tribal Maoris.

There can be no doubt that white New Zealanders are very conscious of their country's Maori past, and of the importance of the Maori community to the nation. But perhaps the Europeans are complacent about the quality of this relationship. For when one speaks to Maoris, one soon discovers that though there is no sense of oppression, there are certainly complaints. The chief of these is that Maoris feel many social avenues are closed to them—in fact, if not by law. Maoris are indeed found in the civil service and the professions, and of course in the army and in agriculture. But not many are to be found in banks, insurance companies and big corporations, and Maoris hint at a still-surviving color bar.

To this the *pakeha* replies that if Maoris of equal quality offered their services, they would be employed. Alternatively, he maintains that Maoris are not ambitious in the European sense and do not in fact wish for the kind of job they say is refused to them. He adds that family and tribal ties mean much more to a Maori than does the typically European urge to individual success. There seems some truth in this, for what is, precisely, attractive in the Maori is his sense of community sharing, his devotion to his family even if this involves material loss, and his instinct to fully enjoy a good life—qualities which the European drive of ambition may inhibit or deny. And indeed, since the Maori slogan is "integration without assimilation," this would seem to imply that these people wish to preserve their own culture in ways that must mean a rejection of some aspects, at least, of European life.

THE Maoris will also tell you that the famed lack of prejudice of the white New Zealander is not without exceptions. They point to the disturbances over racial mixing in the schools at Pukekohe in 1952, called "New Zealand's Little Rock," and to the fact that the country's champion Rugby team is willing to include Maoris when it visits Europe but not when it goes to South Africa. It is only just to add that white protests against this exclusion were equally vehement—if unsuccessful.

Perhaps what one could most reproach white New Zealanders with is not rejection of the Maori but indifference to him. Certainly, white New Zealanders are proud of "their" Maoris, but often in an uninformed and sentimental way. A striking instance is that only about 200 *pakehas* have ever bothered to learn Maori, which is by no means a difficult language, though perhaps one should add that only half of the Maoris speak their own language themselves.

The vast majority of New Zealand place names are still Maori. All these names have a meaning, and white New Zealanders use them every day, yet few of the *pakehas* know the significance of the names they use. Thus, near the celebrated thermal spa of Rotorua, there is a renowned Maori village called Whakarewarewa. In Maori this means "place of rising steam." But though all white New Zealanders know the place, few seem to know what it means, and in any case they generally abbreviate it to "Whaka," which is a Maori prefix with so many meanings as to have none at all, and is certainly less poetic, let alone accurate, than the true Maori name.

TO meet, the Maoris are confident, courteous, intelligent and at first rather reserved. They have great natural dignity, and a pride in themselves and their people which commands respect. But when relaxed, they are great wits and, if highly educated, ready to discuss themselves and their problems critically and without inhibition. The men are strong, virile and graceful, and the girls often beauties, while the elder people have a striking nobility of demeanor. Their dancing is of great plastic grace, and though their ancient art of wood carving is in decline, the intricate convolutions of their traditional designs and the fierce, almost "Oriental" masks of their figure carving make this art one of the finest of Polynesia. Most attractive of all is that, while maintaining their individuality, they have a sense of social obligation and devotion to their fellows which Europeans everywhere have largely lost.

Although there can be no doubt that the European arrival profoundly harmed the Maoris, there is also much evidence to suggest that the Maori civilization was already declining when the Europeans came. Ferocious civil wars racked the country, and oral Maori poetry of the period is a continual story of disaster and lament. It could even be maintained that the European eruption created the Maori nation, since before this time the only loyalty was to the tribe; and indeed, the very word "Maori" does not connote a nationality but simply means "normal." One may also reflect that *somebody* was bound to arrive, sooner or later, to occupy the country with the Maoris, and that in the descendants of the original white New Zealanders they have as sympathetic a group of fellow countrymen as could be hoped for. And from the point of view of the white New Zealander, the presence of the Maori makes possible a more varied culture based on a creative tension between the races.

An instructor teaches the English names of familiar objects to young aborigines at the Ernabella Mission Station in South Australia.

Enlightened Approaches to Peaceful Integration

In both Australia and New Zealand, the early white immigrants from Britain encountered a native population. Following a period of harsh treatment in the 19th Century, each Government has sought to deal fairly with its particular minority group. Australia has the more difficult problem to solve because the aborigines are among the most primitive people on earth. In New Zealand, however, the initially more advanced Maoris have adopted many Western ways and are assuming a major role in the national life.

CAREFUL ARTISAN named Nyukana decorates greeting cards with traditional designs for the Ernabella Mission in South Australia. Profits from native crafts help support the mission.

ABORIGINES on a mission station live partly in their primitive tribal past and partly in the complex modern world

A CORROBOREE, or native festival of chants and dances, is held at Ernabella by male aborigines who beat sticks on the ground. Festivals are either for ritual purposes or for pleasure.

CRUDE HUT thatched with spinifex bushes *(opposite)* near Ernabella houses Walter Pukutiwilinya and his wife Topsy. As she spins yarn for the craft center, Walter plays with the baby.

STOCKMAN ALOFT, Stan Doomadgee eats lunch *(left)* on an airplane taking him to a cattle station. Many sheep and cattle stations depend for their survival on aboriginal stockmen.

HUNTING FOR SMALL GAME, aboriginal children from the Ernabella Mission scramble over rocks in search of rabbits and goanna lizards as well as roots and grubs. Working together, the children surround their animal prey and often catch it by hand; adult aborigines usually use boomerangs for hunting.

DIGGING FOR WATER, children scoop sand out of a dry creek bed *(right)* near the Ernabella Mission Station. In periods of drought, the natives know exactly where to dig for water three or four feet down in the sand. Many aborigines are fair-haired and comparatively light-skinned until they attain adulthood.

WOODEN FIGURES of fabled Maori lovers Tutanekai *(left)* and Hinemoa embrace each other above a gate at Whakarewa-rewa, a model fortified village on New Zealand's North Island.

The legend tells how Hinemoa, forbidden by her tribe to see her lover Tutanekai, swam at night to the island where he lived, buoyed up by gourds and guided by the sound of his flute.

MAORI LEADER, Sir Eruera Tirikatene stands on the steps leading to Parliament House in Wellington, the capital of New Zealand. Sir Eruera is the senior Maori member of Parliament.

MASTER CRAFTSMAN, Pakake Leonard *(below)* is surrounded by some of his highly regarded carvings in his workroom in Rotorua. He plans to start a school for teaching the ancient art.

THE MAORIS retain their old customs while mixing freely in the society of New Zealand

COSTUMED TROUPE of Maori girls performs a traditional dance in the Regent Theatre in Rotorua. Recently formed, the company has danced at festivals in New Zealand and abroad.

Brawny members of lifesaving clubs march resolutely in a surf carnival at Maroubra Beach near Sydney. The clubs compete each summer

weekend in surfing, sea rescue, and boat and swimming races.

Triumphs in Sport

IN sport, Australians and New Zealanders are like two Davids conquering a whole host of powerful Goliaths. Australia wins the Davis Cup 11 times, routing the might of the United States. In swimming, its young champions win 14 out of 23 gold medals at the 1956 Olympics and soon break almost every freestyle record. John Landy of Australia, visiting America, runs two four-minute miles within one week; for years the mile run is dominated by Landy's countryman Herb Elliott; later Peter Snell of New Zealand chops the world mile record down to an incredible 3 minutes 54.4 seconds. The Australian cricketers trounce the English, who invented this peculiar game. The New Zealanders' All Blacks Rugby football team overcomes the famous Springboks of South Africa, routs the fanatical French and cleans up every top team in the British Isles.

How do they do it? How do these countries of insignificant population confront and defeat the athletes of nations so much richer and so much bigger?

To begin with simple reasons, the climate is right for year-round outdoor sporting activities, and these are both readily available and inexpensive. The dietary standard of both countries is excellent. Almost all the people of each nation are participants in sports, not just spectators. The youthful age groups are larger than in most countries, so that a greater number of potential athletes are available than the total population figures might suggest.

But there are deeper reasons. Because these are classless societies, economic background is no obstacle to success, as it might be, for instance, in the United Kingdom. The coaching is methodical and intelligent while not overburdened with theory; and the athletes—those lazy, lackadaisical young Aussies and Kiwis!—submit themselves willingly to training programs of spartan rigor. Then again, there is the undoubted aggressive instinct of both peoples. It is not exactly that they always "play to win" at any cost, but that they are unforgiving of failure and ready to learn from their mistakes. Most of all, these young nations turn their very smallness and remoteness to advantage. Does the greater world ignore Australia and New Zealand? Okay! say the Aussies and the Kiwis. Let them meet us in the sporting arena, man to man, and we'll plurry well show them who's small, or remote, or insignificant!

AUSTRALIANS seem almost human fishes, and swimming, even more than tennis, is a sport in which they have long excelled. The great precursor of this success was Andrew "Boy" Charlton, who, by dramatically defeating a reigning European champion, made the sport enormously popular in his country throughout the 1920s. His victory made him a national hero, so that to do well in this sport became the dream of many young Australians.

There is almost no other sport in which it is possible for the very young to win. And throughout the latter half of the 1950s, a crop of extraordinary Australian youngsters emerged, some of them defeating all aquatic rivals while barely in their teens. Murray Rose, at the age of 17, was a triple gold medalist in the Melbourne Olympics of 1956; and four years later in Rome he broke his own Olympic record for the 400 meters at the advanced age, for a competitive swimmer, of just 21. A handsome, blond six-footer, Rose has always been a vegetarian, and drives himself through the water on a diet that includes

raw vegetables, seaweed jelly and sunflower seeds.

A phenomenal pair are Jon and Ilsa Konrads, children of a Latvian-born dental mechanic. At 15 Jon Konrads held six world records, and at 13 his sister Ilsa held two. Jon's greatest triumph was in 1960 at Rome, when he broke the Olympic record for the 1,500 meters with a timing of 17 minutes 19.6 seconds.

BUT the greatest Australian prodigy is Dawn Fraser, who has swum faster than any other woman in the world and who, among countless exploits, won the 100 meters in Rome in a record 61.2 seconds and later swam this distance in less than a minute. Dawn was born of a working-class family in a Sydney suburb and suffered from severe colds and asthma as a child. Under the guidance of her coach, Harry Gallagher, she achieved both strength and proficiency. Of Amazonian build today, she can chop wood and lift weights with the sturdiest of male athletes, but in recognition of her essential femininity her countrymen have named a daffodil in her honor.

Such achievements have not been possible without devoted training supervised by expert coaches. Jon and Ilsa Konrads were trained by a famous coach named Don Talbot (known to his colleagues as "Ming the Merciless"), who relies on a program of weight lifting and punishing workouts in the pool. Two other coaches who are making Australia's victories possible are John Devitt and Forbes Carlile. Devitt, now retired from racing, was Australia's Olympic swimming captain in 1956 and again in 1960, the year he beat the world records for the 100 meters and 110 yards. Forbes Carlile is a "scientist-swimmer," with a master's degree in science from the University of Sydney, who became scientific adviser to the 1960 Olympic team. In his laboratory the future champions are examined by blood tests to determine general fitness and by an ergometer to gauge capacity for work. He repeatedly measures their lung capacity and pulse rate.

In tennis, the other sport in which Australians are internationally renowned, the key figure is once again a coach, Harry Hopman. Since his appointment as nonplaying captain in 1950, Hopman has seen his team win the Davis Cup on 11 occasions. Small wonder·that in 1953, when his "twins," Ken

Rosewall and Lew Hoad, successfully defended the Cup against the United States, America's Tony Trabert declared that "we were beaten by two babies and a fox." This "fox" is a controversial figure, said by some to be a martinet and fitness crank with no sense of public relations, and by others a thoughtful strategist devoted to his players. What no one can deny is an astonishing success against the U.S.A.

The galaxy of Australian tennis talent is dazzling. Frank Sedgman, who was only 11 when Hopman discovered him in 1939, remains one of the most memorable figures of the stupendous 1950s. With his dramatic service and magnificent all-round play, and his impeccable manners on and off the court, he led the drive that took Australia to the top, and by 1952 he was the finest amateur player of his time. Of 28 Davis Cup matches he lost only three, and in 1951 he became the first Australian ever to win the U.S. singles title. Despite nationwide clamor and a gift of $13,260 made by tennis enthusiasts to his fiancée in the hope that he would stay amateur, he was captured in 1953 by the American tennis promoter Jack Kramer, and became the first of the Australian greats to join the Kramer troupe.

Another powerful player is Lew Hoad, who first played for his country on the Davis Cup team in 1952, when he was 18, remained on the team until 1956, and won the Wimbledon men's singles two years in succession. In 1957 Hoad also turned professional, and though Kramer's guarantee to him of $140,000 for 14 months' play was considered a high one, he succeeded in earning the entire amount in the first three months. A dramatic player with an invincible backhand, he is today, like Sedgman, a substantial and respected citizen. The left-hander Rod Laver became in 1962 the first player since America's Donald Budge to win the "grand slam"—

victories in the singles championships of Australia, France, Britain and America all in one year.

What is the attitude of Australians to their best amateurs turning professional? In general, it is not censorious. Even in the heyday of amateur tennis, the early 1950s, industrial firms and other concerns subsidized the players liberally in the form of jobs. The opposition to professionalism comes from the Lawn Tennis Association of Australia which, in its desire to control the prestige-winning championships of the game, has generally opposed the idea of holding "open" tournaments of all the best players, amateur and professional. The question of a possible "open" championship was recently debated once again—and rejected—by the LTAA.

In track and field, the reputation of the two countries has been advanced by outstanding long-distance runners like John Landy, Herb Elliott and the New Zealander Peter Snell. Landy ran sub-four-minute miles on six occasions between 1954 and 1956. Herb Elliott, who held the mile record for four years after Landy's retirement, evolved a formidable match-winning strategy. In pre-Elliott days, the approved technique was to start fast, coast during the middle laps and then sprint the last few hundred yards. But Elliott's will and stamina enabled him to run the whole race at an accelerating pace, so that he won it, in effect, in the middle of the course, because the sprinters could not overtake his lead despite their greater speed in the final burst to the tape. But later the volatile Kiwi, Peter Snell, cracked Elliott's mile record and became the unbeatable one.

Yachting is another sport in which Australians are trying to break into the international arena. In 1959 Sir Frank Packer, a Sydney publishing and television baron, leased the American 12-meter yacht *Vim*, which, though it had been beaten by *Columbia* in

---

CRICKET'S FAMOUS DON BRADMAN

The greatest player in the history of cricket, according to many experts, was Australia's Sir Donald Bradman. A good fielder and a brilliant tactician of the game, Bradman was a terror at bat and, starting in 1930, led Australian teams to repeated victories over Great Britain in what amounts to the World Series of cricket, the Test Matches. Small and wiry, he could lash the ball to all corners of the field hour after hour—in fact, day after day. He became Australia's greatest popular hero and was knighted in 1949 for his prowess. During his career Bradman scored 117 "centuries" (100 or more runs during one turn at bat) in games against first-class competition. This is equivalent, perhaps, to a lifetime batting average of .400 in major-league baseball. During his first Test Match he reeled off successive scores of 254, 334 and 232. On one occasion he made 452 runs without being put out. His career total, before he retired in 1948, was 27,984 runs.

1958, was still valuable to the Australians since it was well designed and since no 12-meter had ever been built in the country. Australian boats raced in practices against *Vim,* and in 1962 Sir Frank and his syndicate, who had invested $675,000 in their endeavor, took the 12-meter *Gretel* to the United States to compete for the America's Cup. Though the Australian boat was defeated by America's *Weatherly, Gretel's* feat of winning one of the races—the first foreign boat to do so since 1934—aroused Australia's determination to try for the Cup again.

HORSE racing is a veritable passion in Australia, and the classic Melbourne Cup rivals the Epsom and Kentucky Derbys. Small wonder, then, that Australian jockeys have made an international mark. Rae Johnstone, Edgar Britt and Scobie Breasley have been champions as well known in Europe as in their native land. Their success would seem to be due both to the eagerness of apprentice riders in this horse-rearing and horse-loving country and to the strictness with which these lads are trained to judge pace and ride their mounts exactly to a predetermined time.

Australians also excel in sports peculiar to their country or to the British Commonwealth. The chief of these is cricket, and it may seem surprising that this sedate and thoroughly English game should have aroused such passions among the lively Aussies —and produced in Sir Donald Bradman one of the greatest batsmen of all time. Truth to tell, cricket, as a summer sport, is now declining in Australia in favor of tennis, swimming and surfing, but the Aussies can still defeat not only the experienced English but those deft practitioners of this ancient game, the volatile West Indians. Perhaps the appeal of the game to Australians has been twofold. It has been a means of showing the English that Junior could beat Mum at her favorite sport. It also is a far tougher game than it may appear to the casual spectator. For it demands enormous stamina, a strong strategic sense and the nerve to stand up to fast bowlers who hurl an extremely hard, leather-covered ball at the batsman at more than 80 miles an hour.

The Australians play no less than four different varieties of football—the varieties depending more or less on the player's temperament and on the state he happens to live in. Australian Rules, which is chiefly played in the southern states, is the only game Australians have actually invented. There are 18 men to a side, the ball is oval and, although the game is not so spectacularly violent as American football, it is fast and rough, and involves physical stamina and prowess more than tactical subtlety.

Soccer (also called association football), the great game of Europe and Latin America, has only recently been catching on in Australia. That it has made any progress at all is due largely to the immigrant population, so that a champion "Australian" team may consist chiefly of Slavs and Latins with exotic-sounding names. The remaining games are two versions of English Rugby football, but in these the Australians seldom rival the formidable New Zealanders.

FROM the point of view of international reputation, it is a pity that the game in which New Zealand sensationally excels—that of Rugby Union football—is not universally played. New Zealand's chief rivals in this sport are South Africa, France and the peoples of the United Kingdom, and against these nations the country's triumphant All Blacks (so called because of the color of their garments) have won, since their founding more than half a century ago, a resounding and rarely broken series of victories. To those who do not know Rugby Union, one might say it is a mixture of a fast-moving gymnastic performance and a gladiatorial display, involving speed, strategy and formidable sinew. To see the All Blacks in operation against the no less dynamic Springboks of South Africa, or against a British team at the mecca of the sport in Twickenham, England, is to understand the ferocity and determination that underlie the reserved amiability of the Kiwi character.

New Zealand has some 223 peaks more than 7,500 feet high, and in mountaineering its countrymen have won world fame. Sir Edmund Hillary was one of the two climbers who first scaled the world's highest mountain, Everest, and in 1957-1958 he led the first journey made by tracked vehicles to the South Pole. Indeed, the sports in which the New Zealanders excel are not so much the conventional competitive games as those outdoor activities which are directly concerned with nature. There is fishing, especially surf casting for snapper and "game hunting" for swordfish, marlin and shark. In the profusion of gulfs, landlocked harbors, fiords and inland lakes, there is yachting, often in specially designed craft. Almost a public duty is the hunting of noxious animals like deer, which, having been introduced from abroad and having no native predators to devour them, contribute to erosion by destroying mountain vegetation. In horse racing, New Zealand rivals Australia, which sends eager buyers to its bloodstock sales. Truth to tell, the Kiwi obsession with racing is not exclusively athletic, since $50 per head of population is wagered on horses every year.

The older generations are powerfully addicted to the game of lawn bowls, which is played on immaculate swards that are mowed and rolled with loving care. When the players invade a city for a tournament, one may see hundreds of purposeful middle-aged men in impeccable flannels and club blazers, accompanied by bevies of formidable ladies —who often can also swing a deadly ball. A curiosity that should not be neglected—if perhaps it is not exactly a sport—is represented by New Zealand's Marching Girls. These legions of stalwart young ladies, bedecked with vivid tunics, boots and jaunty shakos, perform complex evolutions on public occasions with an air of dedicated paramilitary zeal.

IN both countries the visitor grows to feel that the proximity of most of the people to the sea, coupled with a splendid climate, has much to do with the profusion of sporting prowess. For Australians and New Zealanders largely "live in the water," and there could be no better training for any sports, from earliest youth, than the open-air beach life of these countries. And of this beach life the characteristic feature is the surf carnival, which may be seen as both the genesis and the symbol of these nations' sporting achievements.

Of the many carnivals held in Australia, the most important is the annual nationwide competition. On a broad beach washed by mighty rollers, a crowd perched on makeshift grandstands gathers to watch the carnival's first event: the march past of the lifesaving teams. This is heralded when the band on the beach strikes up the national anthem and the royal standard is run up over the central pavilion. Then, from the far end of the beach, a procession marches along the shore: teams from the six states of Australia and from innumerable lifesaving clubs. Preceded by flamboyant triangular banners of vivid (and, it must be added, often hideous) hues, the champions, all dressed in archaic shirted bathing suits and caps of the same color as their flags, stride on, carrying their rescuing reels and lines. Their pace is stately —how unlike the usual Aussie slouch!—and the rhythmical cohesion of their movements, while not exactly military, expresses an absolute physical and mental unison.

AT length, in their hundreds, they are all lined up along the beach, the breakers thundering behind them and the audience rising to its feet upon the rickety grandstands. The men now perform exercises of lifting and lowering their rescue reels while judges in white flannels and Panama hats—old lifesavers themselves—pass among them searching for finer points in their maneuvers. Then, at a given signal, the athletes advance in a phalanx up the beach, finally pausing before the Governor-General's dais. There is something almost pagan in this spectacle, as if this were a gathering of young warriors parading to reassure the populace before embarking on some antique war.

The key event of the ensuing carnival is the rescue and resuscitation, or R. and R. Since the surf lifesaving clubs were founded in Australia some 60 years ago, nearly 150,000 swimmers have been rescued by the lifesavers; and today, with far more people in the water, there are 223 clubs in the country whose members rescue more than 4,500 swimmers every year. Considering that these men are unpaid volunteers, this is a wonderful achievement. Cynics declare that the lifesavers are physical puritans excessively devoted to the cult of the body beautiful— but perhaps they do not say this when they themselves are rescued. Of course, the lifesaving display at a carnival is in some sense artificial since one member of the team of six who is called the "patient" and who swims out first, later to be "rescued" by the beltman, two linesmen, the reelman and the resuscitator, is in reality a powerful fellow in little need of "rescue."

There is nothing artificial, however, about the possibility of danger in the waters. Throughout the carnival a monoplane circles overhead, looking out for sharks, for the presence of these monsters is an additional hazard to that of the pounding waters. Every year in Australia there are casualties, and the sharks—tiger, gray nurse and whaler—are known to enter small bays and even rivers, and to penetrate the nets intended to protect such surfing beaches as may have them. What is remarkable is that this risk is taken entirely for granted. Unless a roving shark has been spotted and the sea cleared of bathers, the swimmers go in with no more thought of danger than a pedestrian has about being run down by traffic.

The most exciting event for the spectator is without doubt the surfboat races. These light, stalwart craft are manned by four oarsmen and a helmsman who remains standing throughout the race. The men line up on the beach; then when the gun fires they leap to their boats and tug them out toward the boiling surf. Catastrophe soon overtakes some of the craft when they fail to surmount the first breaker, rise vertically and tumble into a turmoil of beating froth. But some boats maneuver breaker after breaker and, disappearing from time to time in deep troughs, succeed in reaching the distant buoys beyond the rollers, where they turn for the home run. It is now that skill is so important. If they catch a roller at precisely the right moment, they can ride it and, by deft steering as it breaks, be carried triumphantly at great speed right up to the beach edge itself. It is an exhilarating spectacle when they achieve this.

THE related phenomenon of surfboard riding is not, of course, exclusive to Australia, and the pioneer who introduced the sport to Sydney, as long ago as 1915, was Duke Kahanamoku from Honolulu. But it is now a highly regarded sport among Aussies, especially since Bernard "Midget" Farrelly won the 1963 international title at Makaha, Hawaii, against the American and Hawaiian champions. A board costs up to $124, and it is estimated that 45,000 are used in Sydney alone.

The individual surfing is a less dramatic, if more graceful, part of the carnival than the lifesavers' surfboat races. The surfers weave, twist and glide among the breakers, looking infinitely fragile as they crouch upon the slender boards on the slopes of rollers that tower above them, yet seeming to win by their art the ease and joy of flight itself.

WHEN the carnival is over, and dusk falls, a rather less serious type of surfer emerges, arousing the ire of the expert performers, who feel his type brings discredit on their cherished sport. These are the "surfies," whose cult originated in the United States, and who are now familiar figures on the Australian shores. A "surfie" probably has some rudimentary skill upon a wave, but his chief ambition is to be a sort of outdoor beatnik. The boys wear patterned Bermuda shorts and usually nothing else—except perhaps a pair of "thong" sandals on their feet —tint their hair electric blond with lemon juice, paste superfluous sunburn cream on their faces and adopt the air of a devil-may-care marine Tarzan. Their girls have wind-swept hairdos, wear skintight trousers and walk in chattering groups often separate from their men. Soon, beneath arc lamps hung along the beach, and to the strains of American "surfie" music, these "kooks" (beginners) and their "femlins" (girl friends) begin their "stomp" upon the beach: a ritual dance of frenetic stamping and gyrating with much waving of the arms.

But these frolics cannot efface the memory of the carnival and what it means. Australians have no tradition of ceremonial and, since they are among the most informal peoples in the world, despise both regimentation and any tribute of respect by means of display. But in a surf carnival one may see a pageant mounted with immense dexterity and style. And since the rescue displays are deemed the most important event of all, these carnivals also underline the people's sense of communal obligation, a survival of the pioneering spirit, whereby the highest civic duty is to succor a neighbor, even a stranger, in distress. Thus one may see how the national worship of health, courage and physical strength receives, in the surf carnival, a symbolic manifestation; and how, in Australia, a physical event can take on an almost spiritual intensity.

Athletes catch their breath at half time in Melbourne during a game of Australian Rules football, a violent, freewheeling sport.

The Serious Pleasures of Sports-minded Nations

Australia and New Zealand are among the most athletic nations in the world. In proportion to their small populations, they have won an astounding number of international sporting events, and most of their celebrities known abroad are athletes. The sunny climate, widespread participation and tough coaching largely explain the athletic successes of both nations. Starting with compulsory sports in grade school, the average child spends many hours of every week achieving physical strength and skill.

SURFBOAT RACE near Sydney reaches a dramatic moment as two boats, nearly swamped by a breaker, almost collide. While four oarsmen *(left)* pull against the rushing surf, their helmsman *(right, center)* tries to guide them clear of the other floundering boat. The object of these races, held at weekend surf carnivals, is to buck the waves and reach a line of buoys far from shore,

and then head back, riding gigantic rollers. Many boats capsize when they meet the first wave, and only strength, skill and a sense of timing can prevent their going under. Because these boats are too hard to maneuver for most rescue missions, a lifeguard generally ties himself to a light line and swims out. When he reaches the victim, both are reeled in to shore.

CRICKET LESSON absorbs promising students during a demonstration of bowling (throwing) at Lindsay Hassett's school in Melbourne. Australia, England's major rival in cricket, usually wins the world championship.

SWIMMING COMPETITION near Sydney at Bronte Beach *(opposite)* takes place in a harborside pool marked off into lanes and filled by the tide, while in the background casual surf swimmers take a dip in the ocean.

TENNIS NEOPHYTES receive instruction *(right)* from Don Tragonning in Melbourne. In Australia, tennis is not as genteel a sport as elsewhere; crowds are knowledgeable and root for their favorites with wild abandon.

TOP ATHLETES command international respect and set a high standard for beginners

DAWN FRASER, considered the greatest woman swimmer in history, pauses in a pool in Melbourne. She swam the 100-meter freestyle in 59.5 seconds in 1962, a world record for women, and has won nine gold medals in two Olympic Games and two British Empire Games. She is a native of Sydney.

HERB ELLIOTT nears the finish line *(right)* as he wins the 1,500-meter event at the 1960 Rome Olympics. Elliott ran sub-four-minute miles 17 times in his career, and at one time held the mile world record. An Australian, he retired in 1962 at the age of 23 to study science in England.

LEW HOAD, the Australian tennis star *(opposite)*, shows his powerful backhand at Wimbledon, where he won the men's singles in 1956 and 1957. In 1956 he triumphed in all three of his Davis Cup matches and took the Australian and French tennis titles. He now plays professionally.

PETER SNELL, who succeeded Elliott as the world's fastest miler when he clocked 3 minutes 54.4 seconds in 1962, trains *(below)* in the rugged hills above Christchurch in his native New Zealand. Possessed of enormous stamina, he runs 100 miles cross country every week while training.

9

The Surprising Artists

YOUNG countries are chiefly concerned with pioneering, creating wealth and establishing their very existence—essential activities that leave small room for art. But what is surprising about Australia and New Zealand is how early in their histories significant artists emerged, and the degree of public support that they so soon achieved. Perhaps the explanation is that new peoples have a strong impulse to understand their surroundings and themselves, and thus achieve a national identity. Indeed, the very lack of tradition can be turned into an advantage. In older countries, artists have defined man and nature for centuries, and for later thinkers there can never be again the same excitement of a first discovery. But

in new lands, the artists can undertake a pioneering task of definition.

At first, the writers and painters of Australia and New Zealand were still shackled by their European pasts and described the new countries in terms they remembered from the old. Thus, colonial poetry and painting, though they have a topographical and historical interest, reveal little of what the new countries and their inhabitants were really like. But from the turn of the 20th Century, a remarkable change ensued when the artists began really to look, ponder and explain. And they succeeded so well that it is not too much to say that they made a second discovery of their countries. The explorers and settlers had opened up the land; the artists revealed its shape and inner spirit.

Though Australia has fine writers, painting is its really characteristic art, while in New Zealand the writers are far more outstanding than the painters. The breakthrough in Australia took place in the late 1880s. A group of young painters joined forces and talents at a village near Melbourne called Heidelberg, to create the "Heidelberg School," which was the first authentically Australian style of painting. These artists have sometimes been called Impressionists, though in the purely pictorial sense they were not so at all. What they borrowed creatively from Impressionism were its light-filled colors and the practice of painting familiar outdoor scenes in a lively and informal manner. What they added was a clear, penetrating, affectionate gaze at the Australian landscape. Before the Heidelberg painters went to work, Australia was, pictorially, a colony of Europe. After them, it was possible for the public and later painters to understand the wild, disordered beauty that is peculiar to the continent.

THE finest of these young painters was Tom Roberts (1856-1931). Placed beside the masterpieces of European landscape art, a Roberts picture may seem a minor achievement—even though, by the rare quality of his sensual paint, it could confront these classic pictures without shame. But never before had any artists tried to capture the weird beauty of Australia with such assurance and imagination. *The Breakaway*, of 1891, is an Australian classic. In this canvas we see a stockman on horseback galloping to prevent a stampede of sheep. The landscape of flat paddocks and casual eucalypti may seem nondescript. But Roberts has seen and felt it with such factual, poetic intensity that the dry acres and shapeless gums are invested with a lyrical magic which is instantly compelling. And in his theme—that of the stockman who seeks to make the huge outback acres his dominion—he has created an image which, for Australia, has the quality of a legend.

Even more varied and accomplished at inventing Australian legend is a contemporary painter, Sidney Nolan. His technique has not the purely painterly beauty of Tom Roberts'—it is indeed so dazzling and hypnotic that, when seeing a Nolan picture, one has almost the feeling of watching the work of a film director, even of a conjurer. His finest achievement is to have looked at the jagged red desert areas of central Australia and made their alarming chaos seem comprehensible—ordered and even exquisite. The outback life he has portrayed with sad, witty and poetical fidelity: the holocaust of animal carcasses in droughts, the lost, lonely colonial townships, the dense green mystery of the dank tropical forests. He has re-created history by painting the explorers, the convicts, the bushrangers and the settlers in scenes of epic imagination. It is not too much to say that this one painter has given his country heroic myths that state and explain its past and present.

OF Irish origin, Nolan is a twinkling, thoughtful man, with a poised assurance coming from wide travel, deep reading and the restless experimentation that has fully explored his natural talent. Though he is kind and patient, there are inner fires of anger and even ruthlessness that can blaze forth on occasion. The most cosmopolitan of artists, and perhaps better known outside his country than any fellow painter, he remains intensely Australian in his basic loyalties and cast of mind: pragmatic, adventurous, poetic.

In the work of the finest painter in Australia today, Ian Fairweather, one cannot, as with Roberts or with Nolan, see a recognizably Australian choice of subject. Nor indeed is Fairweather even Australian by birth. He comes from Scotland, has lived long in the Orient and first came to Australia only 30 years ago. But beginning as a figurative painter, he has evolved an abstract style of such harmony and lyrical invention that he has won the high esteem of younger men.

Fairweather lives on Bribie Island, some hours away from Brisbane. To discover him, the visitor must walk through the bush until, in a gulley, he comes upon two large Polynesian-type huts which the artist has built for himself in this wilderness. When Fairweather, bearded and barefoot, emerges from the larger of these Crusoe-like contrivances, he turns out to be a courteous and amiable sage, who listens more than he talks, and from time to time seems to withdraw so far inside himself as to be unaware that he has company. Ian Fairweather translates writings from the Chinese and also executes, usually in *gouache* on paper, vivid calligraphic patterns in muted hues. These are not mere decorations, but translations into line and color of natural objects he has seen, or of thoughts and feelings he has experienced. Perhaps to say the emotion they conjure up is a religious one would best describe them—but religious in a pantheistic, not a doctrinal way.

A hermit-philosopher may seem an unexpected figure to discover in so brash and hedonistic a country as Australia; yet it is evident that Fairweather's withdrawal from the world is not one from life, and that the hut on Bribie Island is an authentic resting place after a long pilgrimage of self-examination and discovery. To younger Australian artists, his example can teach two lessons: that of the full development, in old age, of maturing powers—for Australian artists have so often begun brilliantly and spent their force in middle age—and that of infusing into Australian realism an element of poetic mysticism.

THESE artists are but three outstanding figures among hundreds. In all the big cities, progressive public galleries exist which, since traditional art is now so rare and costly to obtain, have concentrated on building up Australian collections. Dozens of private galleries—unknown a decade or so ago—have sprung up in the big towns and are supported by rich and adventurous collectors. More than 80 artists' prizes are awarded in the country, among which the travel scholarship of $2,912 founded by the American cosmetics manufacturer Helena Rubinstein is one of the most valued. Large corporations commission works and make films about the painters. No doubt the cynic might suspect in these activities elements of public propaganda and private ostentation. But this would be to miss the point. Australians *like* painting, are curious about and receptive to the artists' visions, and back their judgment with their money.

"Australians like painting so much because they are a lazy people," an Australian critic said recently. But if he meant that they like no other arts, his stricture would be unhistorical, for Australian writing is even older than its painting, if less exciting and unusual. One reason, perhaps, is that coming from England, a country of great writers rather than painters, Australians were dominated longer by the English literary tradition; another is that the visual shock of a new country did not inspire the writers

as powerfully as the painters. True, a distinctive note was struck by the writers of the bush ballads of the turn of the century, and in the tender, impressionistic stories of Henry Lawson, collected in his *While the Billy Boils;* but this bush literature, however charming and affectionate, does verge on sentiment and facility. And if we should seek a portrait of Australians as impressive as the painters' vision of Australia, we must look to contemporary writers of greater rigor, intellect and imagination.

JAMES McAULEY, born in 1917, and now a professor of English at the University of Tasmania, is a lucid, astringent figure in Australian writing. McAuley first leaped to fame—if the wrong kind—when, to demonstrate the pretension of much modern poetry, he and a fellow writer hoaxed a literary journal called *Angry Penguins* into publishing the poetic works of one Ern Malley. Unfortunately for the luckless periodical, Ern Malley did not exist, and his "poems" had been concocted by McAuley and his friend out of incongruous scraps of verbiage having no meaning whatsoever. This exploit did not endear McAuley to many literary pundits—nor did his conversion to the Roman Catholic Church and the resolutely antimodernist line he has taken in art.

But McAuley is a man who denies in order to affirm: he states trenchantly what he thinks is not and then as powerfully declares what he believes to be the living reality of man's existence. His poems, satires and religious elegies have a sustained ironic gravity and tenderness, and one cannot read some of his best verses without feeling they have the ring of immortality. And in his "Terra Australis," with its profound sense of the loneliness and peril that beset his country, there are also lines of gentle affirmation:

It is your land of smiles: the wattle
Scatters its pollen on the doubting heart.

The great achievement of McAuley is that into his admiring vision of Australia he has infused an element of imaginative tragedy. Life in Australia, he tells us constantly, is not just the lazy, sun-kissed bliss it is so often made out to be. This golden continent is dark as well as radiant. In appearance, James McAuley is like a young King Lear: ravaged and tortured, but with fine smiling eyes filled with sardonic wit and an unaffected humanity. With such a poet writing and admired, one may feel that Australia's literature and its people have come of age.

Another writer with a strong sense of the dark side of the Australian sun is Patrick White, the novelist and dramatist, perhaps the best-known literary figure outside his own country. He, too, is a priest-like person, with a manner of extreme reserve, an acid wit, but a basic kindness that seems to come from a great sorrow. Born in 1912, he has perhaps been soured by the early neglect of his writing, and this may be explained by his use of experimental techniques, as with the stream-of-consciousness narration used in his first book, *Happy Valley,* by the probing of psychological maladjustment, as in *The Aunt's Story,* and by his devotion to epic themes, as in *Voss,* a book about the inner life of the explorer Leichhardt. These books failed to interest a public which could not at first accept that tragic destinies could be enacted in Australia.

WITH the appearance of a tragic dimension in Australian letters, there has also been a deepening of the quality of criticism. Traditionally, Australian "critics" have been argumentative and partisan, with little scholarship or intellectual rigor. But with the growing maturity of the nation, this is changing fast, and in Robert Hughes, a man still in his twenties, Australia has found a critic of astonishing erudition, intelligence and imagination. Hughes, who comes from an "old" patrician family—for even in young Australia, such governing clans do now exist—is the most amiable and friendly of men, and one of the most alarming to tangle with. And in a country that resents criticism more than most, it is his rare achievement to have swept like a scythe through the artistic jungle, reassessing, defining and encouraging—and in the end, if leaving many bleeding heads, restoring to other men reputations that were long neglected or denied. Thus, Hughes's *The Art of Australia* is not so much a critical survey of the country's arts alone as an evocation of what is fertile, and what is futile, in Australian life.

The theater—as indeed in most countries—is less outstanding in Australia. But neighborhood theaters, presenting "difficult" plays, exist in all the big cities, and the Elizabethan Theatre Trust subsidizes many experimental productions. Among the best-known dramatists are Ray Lawler, whose *The Summer of the Seventeenth Doll* is an allegory of his country and its people awakening from immaturity, and Alan Seymour, whose *One Day of the Year* is a satire on the patriotic sentimentalities surrounding Anzac Day. The Australian Ballet Company has been well worthy of artists like Margot Fonteyn and Rudolf Nureyev when they have appeared with it, though its choreography is not so notable as its dancing.

But it is in opera that Australian artists, throughout the world, have been the most outstanding. Here Nellie Melba was the pacesetter, for the great operatic diva had a worldwide reputation and was, for decades, the most celebrated Australian. Today Joan Sutherland is almost as illustrious, and younger singers from Australia are to be heard at Covent Garden in London.

At a more basic level of musical enjoyment, there is a great deal to say in praise of the folk-singing movement in the country. This may owe much to Pete Seeger and visiting Negro artists from America, but also to a rich fund of authentic Australian folk ballads, which talented young singers are eagerly reviving. Nor do they stop at that, but write their own songs about current political and social events, often in a mood of protest and of satire—as in the lyrics and music of the gifted young singer and guitarist Gary Shearston. Strictly speaking, these modern ballads can scarcely be regarded as "folk" since they are created not, as of old, on sheep runs and in gold mines, but in dim and delightful night spots, such as Sydney's Troubadour. But the social comment is a sign that this art is not archaic, and it is impressive to see dozens of handsome young Australians listening raptly yet critically to the latest musical description of their daily lives.

IT is scarcely surprising that the arts in New Zealand, where the country is so much smaller and less wealthy, should not have received so large a measure of popular support. We shall nevertheless find, when we come to examine New Zealand literature, that its writers have made an even sharper, deeper revelation of their country than have those in the nearby continent; and we shall also find how much more difficult their task has been.

To understand why this is so, we may best listen to the voices of the writers themselves. The poet Allen Curnow speaks of "the idea that . . . our presence in these islands is accidental, irrelevant; that we are interlopers on an indifferent or hostile scene." The poet R. A. K. Mason echoes this lament, and situates his countrymen

> Here in this far-pitched perilous hostile place
> this solitary hard-assaulted spot
> fixed at the friendless outer edge of space.

And then Allen Curnow defines the second problem when he describes "the 'Kiwi'—our word for the patriotic common man—who disapproves, distrusts or despises the personal voice." The poet Charles Brasch sums up the predicament in four simple words when he writes of New Zealand that "distance looks our way. . . ."

What these poets are telling us, then, is that the New Zealand artist senses the "distance" of his country in terms of history and geography and, equally, his "distance" from the "patriotic common man" to whom he must seek to explain it. How did the artists triumphantly overcome these obstacles?

LET us begin with a convenient date, that of the arrival in New Zealand in 1860 of the Englishman Samuel Butler, later to become a noted moral satirist. He stayed there sheep farming for four years, and from his experiences wrote his utopian fantasy, *Erewhon* (an anagram of "nowhere"), which may be said to be the first New Zealand writing of significance—and in a sense a typical one, since, as we have seen, this is a country which has tried hard to build an earthly paradise. Throughout the last century, there appeared a profusion of poems, tales and histories of little value—though one might mention the masterwork of Prime Minister Sir Julius Vogel, since this, too, is about a fantastic utopia of a kind. Entitled *Anno Domini 2000: or, Woman's Destiny*, this preposterous fable describes, among other lunacies, how its heroine, Hilda Richmond Fitzherbert, Duchess of New Zealand, becomes, in the final glowing pages, empress of about half the globe, including portions of the United States.

The first modern writer of importance—and perhaps still the best known outside New Zealand—was Katherine Mansfield (1888-1923), who, though an expatriate for most of her life, said truly that "New Zealand is in my very bones," for the most sensitive and revealing of her Chekhovian stories are set in her native land. But it was not really until the 1930s that distinctive voices were to be heard in New Zealand itself; and from the outset, there were two somewhat distinctive schools—that of Auckland, on the North Island, and of Christchurch, on the South. In the most general way, one might say that the Aucklanders were more concerned with people and with contemporary verse techniques, and the Christchurch school with a more mystical apprehension of the spirit of the land. The endeavors of both were much assisted by the prolific publication of literary magazines, of which *Landfall*, of Christchurch, was the most enduring, and of firms like the Caxton Press, of the same city, which undertook to publish noncommercial works. We should also notice that in 1947 a governmental Literary Fund came into being and has an excellent record of supporting worth-while writers, and that at the University of Otago it is the custom to have a distinguished writer attached to the academic staff.

Of recent years, and at a growing tempo since World War II, poets and novelists of considerable talent, and increasing assurance, have proliferated in the two islands, and also an unusual category of "poet-historians" like Keith Sinclair, author of a brilliant history of his country. And so fertile is the creation of these artists that we may best give the reader an idea of it by describing four characteristic writers.

THE first is the poet James K. Baxter, who, true to his dictum that the poet should be "a cell of good living in a corrupt society," is, despite his fame, employed as a letter carrier at the capital, Wellington. A man of fierce independence, great sensitivity and occasional truculence, Baxter writes oracular and satirical poems which challenge the complacency of all and sundry. A more urbane character is Ian Cross, the novelist, whose economical *The God Boy*, written as if seen through the eyes of a child, has a depth of psychological penetration and a tragic sense that the earthly paradise of New Zealand may be a paradise lost, which make this short novel, despite its author's youth, one of rare maturity in New Zealand letters. Though he is friendly, witty and gregarious, there is a vein of melancholy and reflection in Ian Cross's temperament, so that one feels at times that one is in the presence of a charming extrovert and at others in that of a philosopher-monk.

Maurice Shadbolt, in his collection of stories entitled *The New Zealanders*, has sought, with earnest intuition, to show how inevitably his countrymen are influenced by their natural environment and, by penetrating almost clinically beneath their illusions and pretensions, to demonstrate that New Zealanders are far more complex and frustrated persons than they may suppose. He is particularly deft at creating convincing female characters, and excellent on the realities of the relations between white and dark New Zealanders. The most remarkable critical spirit in the country is E. H. McCormick, a sort of amiable Jonathan Swift, and a man of punctilious scholarship, deadly wit, and a slightly terrifying gift of lampooning the slipshod and portentous in the New Zealand scene. But in private life McCormick is kindly and entertaining, though always sharp-eyed, like some benevolent owl.

Australians and New Zealanders are eager readers, and the bookstores of both countries, in quality and selection, compare favorably with those of any other people. The publishing houses are enterprising, and those of Australia issue more than 800 titles annually, against 600-odd in New Zealand. Not all these books, of course, are of literary merit, and it is also true that many of the 48 publishing houses of Australia are subsidiaries of foreign firms. Yet it is now no longer indispensable, as it was in Katherine Mansfield's day, to publish—and even work—in Europe or America.

THE existence of a literate public naturally depends on the quality of a nation's educational system, and in both countries this is free, compulsory and secular, so far as state schools are concerned. In Australia, private schools, most of which are denominational, account for 24 per cent of the enrollment, and partial governmental support has recently been offered to them. Australia has 10 universities and three university colleges, and New Zealand four and two, the latter devoted particularly to agricultural

studies. The university student enrollment in Australia is 68,000 (more than 3,300 being Asian students, some of them subsidized by the Colombo Plan), and that of New Zealand 18,000. Most striking has been the rapid development of the Australian National University at Canberra, which has both an Institute of Advanced Studies for postgraduate research, comparable to that in Princeton in the United States, and a School of General Studies, largely for undergraduate work. This means that in the young Australian capital there is, at the disposal of the Government, a rich fund of talent in all academic disciplines.

TO this brief account of the cultural situation in each country might be added these final reflections. The first is that, for the artists, the expatriate problem has almost ceased to exist. The earlier artists nearly all felt obliged to learn their crafts and make a reputation far away in Europe, and sometimes stayed there for many years or for good. Later on, in the period of rising national self-consciousness, to become an expatriate was deemed a kind of cultural high treason, and such artists were denounced as rootless sycophants, worshiping at alien shrines. But today—thanks largely to air transport and the greater prosperity of the artists—the tendency is to commute between many worlds and thus, while remaining an Australian or New Zealander, to enrich an artistic achievement by working both at home and overseas.

The next observation is that the artists of both countries often reveal a strange mixture of diffidence and aggression. The diffidence takes the form of supposing that the cultural life of other countries must, by the very fact of being somewhere else, be better; the aggression, of mistakenly supposing that the artistic achievements of the two nations are being undervalued. In reality, as has been suggested, Australian and New Zealand artists have no real ground for either sentiment. It may in truth be said that neither country has yet produced an artist of the highest caliber if judged by the loftiest standards of international art history. Yet in so short a time, and in the face of so many numbing obstacles, the artists of both nations have made a marked impression on their people and even on the outside world.

After an opera performance at the Adelaide Festival of Arts, Australian Prime Minister Sir Robert Menzies departs with his wife.

An Awakening Interest in Artistic Activities

A sense of neglect and of isolation once caused many of the truly creative people in Australia and New Zealand to leave their homelands. In recent years, however, both the public and the Governments have actively supported the arts. In Australia, a large audience follows the work of native writers, artists and performers. The Government-sponsored Adelaide Festival of Arts, which takes place every other year, presents performances of symphony and chamber music, drama, ballet and opera as well as exhibitions of Australian painting. In New Zealand, a proliferation of literary magazines, an active book publishing industry and Government subsidies for writers attest to a continuing ferment in literature.

*AUTHORS have shown keenness
of observation in delineating
the character of their countrymen*

KATHERINE MANSFIELD, the celebrated short-story writer (1888-1923), was a native of Wellington, New Zealand. Stories like "Prelude" and "Bliss" are models of precise, sensitive prose.

PATRICK WHITE, an experimental novelist *(right)*, is the Australian writer best known abroad. Most of his novels, like *Voss* and *Riders in the Chariot*, are set in the bleak outback.

NGAIO MARSH, a New Zealander, is famous for her mystery novels, like *False Scent* and *Final Curtain*. The picture of the Globe Playhouse bespeaks her lifelong interest in Shakespeare.

SYLVIA ASHTON-WARNER, a New Zealand author *(right)*, has drawn upon her years of teaching Maoris in her acclaimed first novel, *Spinster*, and also in her nonfiction work, *Teacher*.

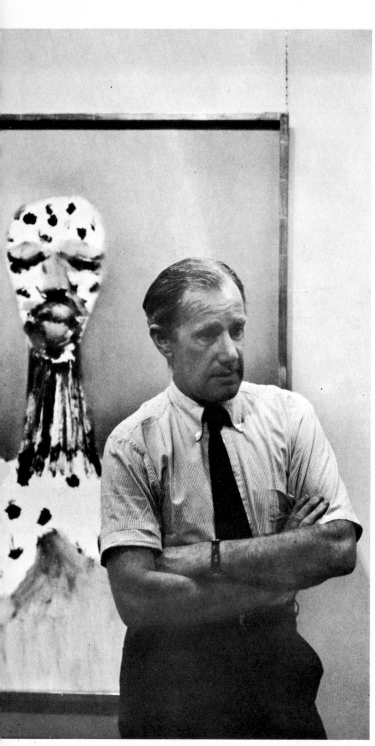

DELICATE VIGOR characterizes the paintings of Australian Sidney Nolan, who applies a controlled technique to primitive subjects. The work behind him portrays an African woman.

MENACING FORMS emerge from the canvases of New Zealand's leading nonobjective painter, Colin McCahon *(right)*. Many of his paintings are scrawled with religious inscriptions.

ARTISTS have discovered individual styles while working in all the current modes of sculpture and painting

ABSTRACT LANDSCAPES executed by Australian painter John Olsen reflect the influence of contemporary American styles upon him and his feeling for the Australian terrain.

MONUMENTAL CONSTRUCTIONS are the work of the young Australian sculptress Norma Redpath. Beside her is the plaster model of *Desert Arch*, which has since been cast in bronze.

PSYCHOLOGICAL INSIGHTS distinguish the portraits of William Dobell, the Australian painter *(right)*. In the background is a powerful, stylized study of a Sydney oil magnate.

Aboriginal stockmen board a DC-3 on Mornington Island, off the coast of Queensland. The airplane flies weekly through northwest

Queensland, conveying passengers and freight to isolated stations.

10

A Search for Identity

AUSTRALIA and New Zealand have conquered poverty and pain, two great evils that afflict so much of the modern world. Their societies are prosperous, sane and energetic, and their peoples healthy, sensible and possessed of a strong sense of community. Their countries, though so different, are beautiful and well loved, and their cities dedicated to the good material life. Then why may one feel that something essential is lacking?

It is not only visitors who may sense this, but many of the more articulate citizens themselves. Both countries are highly self-critical, though they tend to resent—as perhaps all countries do—any criticism from the outside. But it is impossible to read what the writers have said about their nations, or to listen to the more enlightened political, industrial or social thinkers, without becoming aware of a strong feeling that while so much has been achieved, there are also certain areas of sterility and complacency in the national life. Let us try to enumerate some of these strictures, while always remembering that the best kind of Australian or New'Zealander is quite as much aware of them as is anyone else.

An almost fanatical independence in the private sphere tends to accompany a stultifying uniformity in the public sector. As individuals, these people are forthright, reflective and full of character. But in their collective life the tone is often drab, unimaginative and mediocre. Thus, in politics it is striking how few of the best minds and spirits of these nations take any active part. And among trade unions and management one is struck by the number of old men of old ideas who are controlling these young and vigorous countries. Again and again, in all sectors of corporate life, one meets younger men of great intelligence, curiosity and self-awareness who are not in power. And just as frequently, one hears public pronouncements by those in control which seem smug, cautious and backward-looking. The "war of the generations" exists in every nation and nowhere so strongly as in Australia and New Zealand, but in these two countries the public tone is still often set by those who give the impression of being dragged reluctantly into the modern world.

IN foreign affairs, despite the acute awareness of awakened spirits, the two nations have not yet faced the realities of their positions. That England cannot any longer spring to their aid is fully recognized, but the feeling subsists that the United States or someone else will be there in time of trouble and that, in any case, some miracle will occur whereby their shores will automatically be inviolate. A meager defense effort accompanies an ostrichlike belief that all will be well because it always has been.

Indeed, when one considers the military obligations of both countries, one can see that these exceed any present defense capacity to meet them. For both nations have to defend their own shores and their overseas territories, while under the ANZUS (Australia-New Zealand-U.S.) and SEATO (Southeast Asia Treaty Organization) treaties, they must also consult with the U.S. and their Asian allies and take appropriate action if any of them is attacked. In this connection, the very fact that Australian and New Zealand troops have fought in the past with such conspicuous gallantry may mask the need for bearing present burdens. "We did it before, and we can do it again" seems to be the national dogma.

But in modern conditions, will there ever again be time to mobilize against an eventual danger?

In diplomatic terms, one might class Australia's chief external interests as follows: The alliance with the U.S. remains a cornerstone of Australia's external thinking, as is the continuation of the country's connection with the British Commonwealth, though there is a growing skepticism about its value to Australia. In relation to Europe, the chief effort is to ensure that if Britain does ever enter the Common Market, Australian commerce will not be unduly prejudiced, and relations with the Common Market countries are also being assiduously fostered. In relation to Communist China, the tactic is to develop trade relations—though many politicians, believing China to be the ultimate menace, consider that Chinese policy is to entrap Australia into commercial dependence on its wheat and wool markets. Australia also firmly—if not very effectively—supports the new Federation of Malaysia and the pro-Western governments of Southeast Asia, though this conflicts with its most immediate anxiety: to remain on as friendly terms as possible with its nearest neighbor, Indonesia, which has 100 million people and is anti-Malaysia, and whose New Guinean dependency, West Irian, has a land frontier with Australian New Guinea. The foreign policies of New Zealand are largely similar, though it tends to feel more remote, geographically speaking, from Asian affairs.

IN general, it may be fairly said that neither country has yet decided what its attitude must be not so much to Asia as to Asians. Are groups of Asian students to be welcomed as birds of passage under the Colombo Plan? Most certainly. Are large-scale trade relations to be promoted with Japan and even with Communist China? Straightaway. But are Asians to be seen not just as millions of potential consumers living to the north, but as peoples with ancient as well as now-developing cultures? More pertinently, are Asians equals or are they not? The point about this is not that right or wrong answers have been given, but that in this question, vital to both countries, no answer at the profounder emotional levels has yet been found at all. Of course there are Australian theorists who declare that the jet age has taken their country farther out of the Asian orbit than it ever has been before. But with Indonesia just across the Timor Sea, and China looming like a colossus to the north, it is rather hard to give credit to this reassuring theory.

This is not to deny that in the field of foreign aid the record of both countries is a fine one. Since World War II, Australia has given $672 million in overseas aid and provided some $360 million in grants to Papua and New Guinea. Of the foreign aid, $118.7 million has gone to the Colombo Plan, both for capital investment in Asia and for training, in Australia, more than 5,000 subsidized Asian students. New Zealand spends annually some $4.5 million on external aid, of which almost $3 million is allocated to the Colombo Plan. Neither country, by the way, receives any aid from the United States— and both are somewhat distressed to discover that most American visitors believe the contrary.

WITHIN the two nations, the imbalance of town and country, especially in Australia, seems unhealthy. Of course industry demands cities, and of course much of Australia is infertile. But when one sees the thousands of hedonistic young "surfies" on the Sydney beaches, and contrasts their lives with those of the rare young men on the cattle stations of the outback, one cannot but feel—however engaging the "surfies" themselves may be—that Australia has not yet fully confronted its own interior. Nor, in the public sector, can one feel that the national effort to develop the vast rural portions of the continent is, despite all difficulties, imaginative or even adequate. As James McAuley has so aptly put it:

> . . . and though they praise the inner spaces,
> When asked to go themselves, they'd rather not.

As for the urban societies of both countries, what strikes the visitor most is how imitative they are. The architect Robin Boyd has coined the word "Austerican" to describe his country's addiction to so many of the superficial manifestations of American culture; and indeed, one may fairly say that whereas an Australian is immediately recognizable as being himself, and in no way a carbon copy of any other nationality, his social customs consist largely of a 19th Century British foundation with a 20th Century American superstructure. Australians and New Zealanders are, in general, very certain as to what to do but not so certain as to what to think. It is indeed with difficulty that one may discover very many really original ideas in either country that have greatly influenced the nations of the outside world. As peoples, both nations are packed with individuals; as cultures, they remain largely derivative.

A highly attractive quality of both peoples is their profound contempt for fuss, for nice points of protocol and excessive worry. But this sometimes accompanies an attitude which is best enshrined in the national sayings "She'll do" (Australia) and "She'll be right" (New Zealand), which one might describe as a combination of inborn optimism, sloth and indifference to standards. All peoples are perhaps less energetic than they think—and all tend to suppose their neighbors are far lazier than themselves. Nevertheless, the notion that life owes these countries a debt, and that sensational results will be achieved by a minimum effort, is somewhat prevalent in Australia and New Zealand, and is perhaps best symbolized by the Australians' dedication to the "smoke-oh," the interminable break from work which is deemed to be the right of every citizen. Nor, despite the social stability of both countries, are they free from underlying and not always recognized inner tensions. In New Zealand, despite the self-congratulatory tone of racial commentary, the realities of the confrontation with the Maori fellow citizens have not yet been fully accepted. In Australia, the Protestant-Roman Catholic friction remains, at least in certain political and economic spheres.

PERHAPS what most strikes the visitor who comes to Australia or New Zealand from any land with a tragic past or a troubled present is that neither nation seems to be fully aware of its enormous vulnerability. New Zealanders may sense this more because of their small population and almost total reliance on agricultural exports. But Australia, booming, brash and buoyant, seems less to realize that its prosperity and safety are not so much inherent as dependent on the happy conjunction of a series of historical accidents. Traversing this splendid country, with its sun and joy and sports and riches, one may sometimes feel oneself to be in a kind of paradise before the Fall, amid a people committed

A Search for Identity

to a life of mindless beatitude. One cannot imagine Cassandra getting a hearing in Australia, let alone a Moses or a Dante. One cannot even really imagine the existence of a Romeo and Juliet. For in Australia, Cassandra would become a "personality" on television—her warnings treated with tolerant condescension—while Romeo and Juliet would simply tell their Montague and Capulet elders to stop "going crook" about the situation, and themselves go off to Manly beach to join in a surf carnival. These countries have no tragic sense because they believe that they have bypassed tragedy. So far they have, and all good wishes to them; but history is tragic and has few favorites for long.

AND yet, despite its blithe assurance, one may also sense that neither nation is quite yet sure of what it is, and what its destiny. There is a profound renunciation of the past and a straining toward the future, but a gnawing uncertainty as to what form this future can or ought to take. Thus public commentary in these countries, while rejoicing in the good life that fate and their own virtues have bestowed upon them, betrays also an increasing doubt as to the value, stability and direction of their cultures. The finer spirits of both nations are increasingly demanding "What?" and "Whither?"

For it would be a mistake to suppose that beneath the hedonism of these peoples there are not also an unborn idealism and an imaginative capacity to dream large dreams. It is true that these capacities are often marred by a niggling spirit of critical denial in which the admirable laconic realism of the national temperaments is debased into a sour, sterile negation. Brave and generous as these peoples are, they seem sometimes capable of behaving with a mediocrity that belies their true, rare qualities. One has even the impression sometimes that Australians and New Zealanders are reluctant to assume their own greatness, or are unaware of it.

But perhaps they are wise, after all, not to worry overmuch about what they are, but to be ready to discover this empirically by their achievements. And these, beyond question, are impressive. One could cite the agricultural and industrial expertise; the huge increase in recent years of social and commercial sophistication; the assimilation (in Australia) of large alien populations; and the determination to make their countries known in trade, sport and artistic endeavor. Even in the realm of defense, one must concede that if these nations might, at present, be easily invaded, they would be extremely difficult to occupy. Perhaps it is the very fact that Australians and New Zealanders are in such a tearing hurry that may mask from the casual observer their realization that they are ultimately on their own and must themselves find out how to confront this situation.

Nor can anyone visit either country without being immensely seduced by those radiant, forthcoming, life-loving aspects of the Aussie and Kiwi temperaments. Time and again you may be exasperated—as when a hotel will firmly refuse you dinner when you arrive at 7:31 p.m. because the dinner hour is advertised to last only until 7:30. But then you will notice that the very waitress who denies you would have no inhibition whatever about working in domestic service, for Australia and New Zealand must be the only countries of European origin where no shame is attached to performing any kind of manual labor. Or an Aussie or Kiwi in a pub will madden you by his ludicrous yet dogmatic views on world events of which he is totally ignorant, and then say, "Come back to my place and meet the wife and she'll fix you some grog and tucker"—which she indeed does, with genuine and unaffected kindliness. "We're a weird mob," the Australians say, and that goes for the Kiwis too. But what a darn nice mob they are— a "beaut" people, as the Australians would put it.

AT Christmastime in a recent year, a family of British immigrants were lost on the arid, dangerous Birdsville track in central Australia, and though they ultimately perished, the whole nation had in the meantime become obsessed with their discovery and rescue. This concern symbolizes one of the most enduring qualities of both peoples: that they have not, like many more populous nations, lost their sense of community and of the individual's responsibility for his neighbors. And they have one even greater quality, which no criticism can rob them of. Both nations are dedicated to the achievement for all their people, in so far as this is possible, of the most rare and precious quality in any society, which is simply that of human happiness.

An audience gathers on the peaceful campus of Adelaide University to attend a writers' seminar during the Adelaide Festival of Arts.

NEW RESPONSIBILITIES *which threaten their comfortable insularity* . . .

New Zealanders in Christchurch commemorate the landing of their troops in Europe in World War I.

A white-jacketed assistant instructs a Malayan exchange student in a New Zealand botany class.

. . . are drawing Australians and New Zealanders into an increasing consideration

of their involvement in world affairs and their relations with their Asian neighbors

Appendix

HISTORICAL DATES

AUSTRALIA

1606   Australian coast is discovered by Dutch navigator Willem Jansz

1642   Abel Tasman discovers Van Diemen's Land, now Tasmania

1770   Captain James Cook reaches the east coast of Australia, takes possession of New South Wales for Britain

1788   Governor Arthur Phillip establishes first settlement

1791-1801   Whaling begins, coal is discovered, and factories are established to weave wool and mill flour

1802-1803   Matthew Flinders circumnavigates the continent, mapping the coastline

1807   First Merino wool is shipped to London

1810   Governor Lachlan Macquarie inaugurates first big public works

1813   Blaxland, Lawson and Wentworth cross the Blue Mountains

1814   Civil courts are established in Sydney

1824   New South Wales becomes a Crown Colony with appointed legislative council

1825-1836   Van Diemen's Land is proclaimed a separate colony. Settlements are established at present-day Perth, Melbourne and Adelaide

1840-1841   Edward John Eyre makes the first crossing of the continent from east to west

1843   First representative government is established in new South Wales as two thirds of the legislative council is chosen by vote

1851   Gold is discovered in New South Wales and Victoria; a gold rush begins

1853   Abolition of transportation of criminals to Van Diemen's Land, which in this year is renamed Tasmania

1856   Elected legislative assemblies are established in New South Wales, Victoria, South Australia and Tasmania

1860   Burke and Wills cross continent from south to north

1868   Transportation of criminals to Australia is finally abolished

1880   First frozen meat shipment from Australia arrives in England

1883   Federal Council is established and railroad is completed linking Sydney and Melbourne

1897-1898   Federal Convention drafts constitution for federated Australia

1901   Commonwealth of Australia is proclaimed

1908   Canberra is chosen as site of the federal capital

1914   Australia enters World War I, occupies German New Guinea and other German possessions in the South Pacific. Troops leave for the Middle East

1915   Australian divisions suffer heavy casualties in gallant assault on Gallipoli. Several divisions later serve on the Western Front

1917   East-west Transcontinental Railway is opened

1923   Rich mineral deposits are discovered at Mount Isa

1927   First Parliament to meet in Canberra opens

1934   Air-mail route is established between Australia and England via Singapore

1939   Australian military forces are again sent to Middle East as World War II begins

1941-1942   Rapid Japanese conquests threaten Australia and Darwin suffers air attack. U.S. forces arrive. Allies counterattack into New Guinea

1945   Commercial air service is opened between Australia and United States

1946   Government-sponsored immigration program begins

1950   Australian forces serve in Korea

1951   Colombo Plan is launched and ANZUS pact is signed

1954   Southeast Asia Treaty Organization (SEATO) is established

1955-1961   Rapid industrial advances are made as a large refinery, an atomic reactor, a petrochemicals complex, new gas and oil wells, and other industrial establishments are opened

NEW ZEALAND

c.1350   "Great Migration" of Maoris to New Zealand

1642   Dutch navigator Abel Tasman is the first European to discover the country

1769   First of Captain Cook's voyages to New Zealand

1840   Treaty of Waitangi; Maoris cede sovereignty to the Crown. Captain Hobson becomes governor and first of the New Zealand Company's settlers arrive in Wellington

1840-1850   Several settlements are founded, including Nelson, Otago and Canterbury

1852   Achieving self-government, New Zealand is divided into six provinces with a central assembly in Auckland

1860-1872   Series of battles with the Maoris, called the Maori Wars, results from European encroachment on Maori lands

1861   Gold is discovered in Otago

1863   First railroad is opened

1865   Seat of government is transferred to Wellington

1876   Provincial governments are abolished; country is divided into 63 counties

1877   The Education Act provides for free, compulsory and secular education

1879   Adult male suffrage is established

1891   Liberals come into power; sweeping social and industrial legislation is introduced

1893   Women obtain suffrage

1894   Industrial Conciliation and Arbitration Act is passed

1898   Old-age Pensions Act is passed

1907   New Zealand is given Dominion status

1914-1918   World War I; New Zealand Expeditionary Force serves at Gallipoli and on the Western Front

1920   New Zealand joins League of Nations and is given a mandate to administer Western Samoa

1935   Labour Government begins first of four successive terms; wide social legislation

1939-1945   World War II; New Zealand forces are active on all fronts, including the campaigns in North Africa, Italy, Greece, Crete and the Pacific. At war's end New Zealand joins the United Nations

1950   Colombo Conference. New Zealand troops and naval units fight in the Korean War

1951   New Zealand, Australia and U.S. join in ANZUS pact

1954   SEATO treaty is signed

1958   Trade agreement is made with Japan. Sir Edmund Hillary, who climbed Mount Everest in 1953, reaches the South Pole traveling overland

1962   Western Samoa becomes independent. One thousandth Asian student arrives under the Colombo Plan

FOR FURTHER READING

CHAPTER 1: TWO DISTANT LANDS

Barrett, C. L., *Wildlife of Australia and New Guinea*. William Heinemann, Melbourne, 1954.

Duff, R. D., *The Moa-hunter Period of Maori Culture*. Government Printer, Wellington, 1959.

Freeman, J. D., and W. R. Geddes, eds., *Anthropology in the South Seas*. Avery, New Plymouth, 1960.

Laseron, C. F., *The Face of Australia*. Angus & Robertson, Sydney, 1954.

Marlow, B.J.G., *Marsupials of Australia*. Jacaranda Press, Brisbane, 1962.

Moon, G.J.H., *Focus on New Zealand Birds*. Reed, Wellington, 1960.

Troughton, E. Le G., *Furred Animals of Australia*. Angus & Robertson, Sydney, 1957.

CHAPTER 2: HISTORY

Barnard, Marjorie, *A History of Australia*. Frederick A. Praeger, 1963.

Carrington, H., *Life of Captain Cook*. Sidgwick & Jackson, London, 1939.

Clark, Manning, *A Short History of Australia*. New American Library, 1963.

Condliffe, J. B., *New Zealand in the Making*. Allen & Unwin, London, 1959.

Godley, Charlotte, *Letters from Early New Zealand*. Whitcombe & Tombs, Christchurch, 1951.

Hill-Reid, W. S., *John Grant's Journey: A Convict Story*. William Heinemann, Melbourne, 1957.

Oliver, W. H., *The Story of New Zealand*. Roy Publishers, 1960.

Sharp, Andrew, *The Discovery of Australia*. Oxford University Press, 1963.

Shaw, A.L.G., *The Story of Australia*. Faber & Faber, London, 1961.

Sinclair, Keith, *A History of New Zealand*. Penguin Books, 1959.

CHAPTER 3: THE AUSTRALIAN LAND

Australia 1963. Official Handbook. Department of the Interior, Canberra.

Australian Encyclopedia. Grolier Society of Australia, 1962.

Bergamini, David, and the Editors of LIFE, *The Land and Wildlife of Australia*. Time Incorporated, 1964.

Tweedie, Alan D., and Kenneth W. Robinson, *The Regions of Australia*. Longmans, Green & Co., London, 1963.

CHAPTER 4: AUSTRALIAN SOCIETY

Caiger, George, *The Australian Way of Life*. William Heinemann, Melbourne, 1953.

Coleman, P., *Obscenity, Blasphemy, Sedition: Censorship in Australia*. Jacaranda Press, Brisbane, 1962.

Immigration Reform Group, *Immigration: Control or Colour Bar?* Melbourne University Press, 1960.

MacKenzie, Jeanne, *Australian Paradox*. MacGibbon & Kee, 1962.

Price, Charles A., *Southern Europeans in Australia*. Oxford University Press, 1963.

CHAPTER 5: LIFE IN NEW ZEALAND

Condliffe, J. B., *The Welfare State in New Zealand*. Allen & Unwin, London, 1959.

Dollimore, Edward S., ed., *New Zealand Guide*. H. Wise & Co., Dunedin, 1962.

Lipson, Leslie, *The Politics of Equality*. University of Chicago Press, 1948.

McLintock, A. H., *A Descriptive Atlas of New Zealand*. Government Printer, Wellington, 1959.

Mansfield, Katherine, *The Garden Party*. Random House, 1922.

Sinclair, K., *Distance Looks Our Way*. Paul's Book Arcade, Hamilton, 1961.

CHAPTER 6: POLITICS AND ECONOMICS

Arndt, H. W., and W. M. Corden, eds., *The Australian Economy*. F. W. Cheshire, Melbourne, 1963.

Australia, An Economic and Investment Reference. Australian News and Information Bureau, 1964.

Chapman, R. M., *Ends and Means in New Zealand Politics*. Auckland, 1961.

Clark, Colin, *Australian Hopes and Fears*. Hollis and Carter, London, 1958.

New Zealand Monetary & Economic Council, *Economic Growth in New Zealand*. Government Printer, Wellington, 1962.

Sawer, Geoffrey, *Australian Government Today*. Melbourne University Press, 1948.

Westrate, C., *Portrait of a Modern Mixed Economy*. New Zealand University Press, 1959.

CHAPTER 7: ABORIGINES AND MAORIS

Bigwood, Kenneth and Jean, and Harry Dansey, *The New Zealand Maori in Colour*. Reed, Wellington, 1963.

Buck, Sir Peter, *The Coming of the Maori*. Whitcombe and Tombs, Christchurch, 1954.

Elkin, A. P., *The Australian Aborigines*. Angus & Robertson, Sydney, 1961.

Hilliard, N. H., *Maori Girl*. William Heinemann, London, 1960.

McCarthy, Frederick D., *Australian Aborigines, Their Life and Culture*. Colorgravure Publications, Melbourne, 1957.

Mitcalfe, B., trans., *Poetry of the Maori*. Paul's Book Arcade, Hamilton, 1961.

CHAPTER 8: SPORTS DOWN UNDER

Brittenden, R. T., *Great Days in New Zealand Cricket*. Reed, Wellington, 1958.

Gordon, H., *Young Men in a Hurry*. Lansdowne Press, Melbourne, 1961.

Hillary, Sir E. P., *High Adventure*. Hodder & Stoughton, London, 1955.

Jarden, R. A., *Rugby on Attack*, Whitcombe & Tombs, Christchurch, 1961.

Moyes, A. G., *Australian Cricket*. Angus & Robertson, Sydney, 1959.

Pollard, J., *Lawn Tennis, the Australian Way*. Lansdowne Press, Melbourne, 1963.

CHAPTER 9: LITERATURE AND THE ARTS

Baxter, James K., *The Fire and the Anvil: Notes on Modern Poetry*. New Zealand University Press, 1955. *The Iron Breadboard, Studies in New Zealand Writing*. Mermaid Press, Wellington, 1957.

Boyd, Robin, *Australia's Home: Its Origins, Builders and Occupiers*. Melbourne University Press, 1963. *The Australian Ugliness*. Penguin Books, 1963.

Green, H. M., *A History of Australian Literature*, 2 vols., Angus & Robertson, Sydney, 1961.

Hall, H. B., *Ballet in Australia from Pavlova to Rambert*. Georgian House, Melbourne, 1948.

Hope, A. D., *Australian Literature 1950-1962*. Melbourne University Press, 1963.

McCormick, E. H., *Eric Lee-Johnson*. Paul's Book Arcade, 1956. *New Zealand Literature: A Survey*. Oxford University Press, 1959.

McLeod, A. L, ed., *The Pattern of Australian Culture*. Cornell, 1963.

Moore, William, *The Story of Australian Art*, 2 vols. Angus & Robertson, Sydney, 1934.

Mulgan, Alan, *Great Days in New Zealand Writing*. Reed, Wellington, 1962.

Orchard, W. A., *Music in Australia*. Georgian House, 1952.

Simpson, E. C., *A Survey of the Arts in New Zealand*. Wellington Chamber Music Society, 1961.

CHAPTER 10: PRESENT PROBLEMS

Airey, W. T., E. Beaglehole and C.G.F. Simpkin, *New Zealand and the Pacific*. New Zealand Institute of International Affairs, 1947.

Gordon, B. K., *New Zealand Becomes a Pacific Power*. University of Chicago Press, 1960.

Grattan, C. Hartley, *The United States and the Southwest Pacific*. Harvard, 1961.

Greenwood, Gordon, and Norman Harper, eds., *Australia in World Affairs, 1950-1955*. F. W. Cheshire, 1957. *Australia in World Affairs, 1956-1960*. F. W. Cheshire, Melbourne, 1963.

Larkin, T. C., ed., *New Zealand's External Relations*. Oxford University Press, 1962.

Living With Asia. Australian Institute of International Affairs, 1963.

Wood, F.L.W., *New Zealand in the World*. Department of Internal Affairs. Wellington, 1940.

FAMOUS AUSTRALIAN CULTURAL FIGURES AND THEIR PRINCIPAL WORKS

LITERATURE

Furphy, Joseph (Tom Collins)	1843-1912	Panoramic novel of life in the outback: *Such Is Life*
Clarke, Marcus	1846-1881	Novel depicting convict era: *For the Term of His Natural Life*
Paterson, A. B. ("Banjo")	1864-1941	Bush ballads: "The Man from Snowy River," "Waltzing Matilda"
Stephens, A. G.	1865-1933	Literary critic influential in the development of Australian literature
Gilmore, Dame Mary	1865-1962	Poems of compassion: *Fourteen Men*
O'Dowd, Bernard	1866-1953	Poems of exhortation: *The Poems of Bernard O'Dowd*
Lawson, Henry	1867-1922	Short stories reflecting the harsh realities of outback life: "The Drover's Wife," "Water Them Geraniums." Poems
Brennan, Christopher J.	1870-1932	Australia's most profound and powerful poet: *The Verse of C. J. Brennan*
Richardson, Henry Handel (pseud. of Ethel Florence Richardson)	1870-1946	Novels drawing deeply upon personal experience: *The Fortunes of Richard Mahony*
Neilson, John Shaw	1872-1942	Delicate poems capturing elusive moods: *Collected Poems, Unpublished Poems*
McCrae, Hugh	1876-1958	Vigorous, lusty poetry on themes drawn from history and mythology: *The Best Poems of Hugh McCrae*
Franklin, Miles	1879-1954	Novels marked by a strong Australian flavor: *My Brilliant Career, My Career Goes Bung*
Prichard, Katharine	1884-	Novels reflecting concern for social problems: *Coonardoo, Working Bullocks, Haxby's Circus*. Short stories
Palmer, Vance	1885-1959	Poems, novels, short stories and dramas influenced by egalitarian convictions. Novels: *The Passage, Golconda, Seedtime, The Big Fellow*
Boyd, Martin	1893-	Urbane novels on themes of family life: *The Montforts, The Cardboard Clown, A Difficult Young Man, Outbreak of Love*
Dark, Eleanor	1901-	Historical novels: *The Timeless Land, Storm of Time, No Barrier*. Psychological novel: *Prelude to Christopher*
Slessor, Kenneth	1901-	Poems marked by a virtuosity in the use of language: *Poems*
FitzGerald, R. D.	1902-	Poetry on philosophical themes: *This Night's Orbit, Southmost Twelve*
Hope, A. D.	1907-	Love poetry and satires. Influential literary criticism
White, Patrick	1912-	Australia's most experimental novelist, writing on man's search for fulfillment: *Happy Valley, The Living and the Dead, The Aunt's Story, Voss, Riders in the Chariot*. Drama: *The Ham Funeral*
Stewart, Douglas	1913-	Dramas: *Ned Kelly, The Fire on the Snow, The Golden Lover*. Poems, short stories and literary criticism
Wright, Judith	1915-	Lyrical poetry: *The Moving Image, Woman to Man, The Gateway, The Two Fires, Birds*
McAuley, James	1917-	Poems of forceful satire and on religious themes: *Under Aldebaran, A Vision of Ceremony*. Essays: *The End of Modernity*
Lawler, Ray	1921-	Dramas skillfully reproducing Australian patterns of speech: *The Summer of the Seventeenth Doll, The Piccadilly Bushman*

MUSIC

Hill, Alfred	1870-	Composer whose works reflect melodic elements of primitive Maori music
Antill, John	1904-	Composer of works mainly for the stage. His ballet, *Corroboree*, is based on rhythms of aboriginal music

PAINTING AND SCULPTURE

Buvelot, Louis	1814-1888	Painter. Realistic portrayals of suburban farms and settled countryside
Roberts, Tom	1856-1931	Painter of romantic Impressionist scenes of rural life
Streeton, Arthur	1867-1943	Heroic Impressionist landscapes in a style that long influenced Australian landscape painting
Conder, Charles	1868-1909	Impressionist landscapes. Also pioneer of *art nouveau* style
Long, Sidney	1872-1955	Etchings and *art nouveau* landscapes
Preston, Margaret	1883-	Decorative still lifes and landscapes
Fairweather, Ian	1890-	Inventive, semiabstract paintings influenced by Oriental art
Miller, Godfrey	1893-	Allegorical paintings in which color and form continuously fluctuate under the influence of energy and light
Herman, Sali	1898-	Painter. Joyful, sensuous depictions of commonplace scenes
Dobell, William	1899-	Painter of revealing, sometimes sardonic portraits
Passmore, John	1904-	Subtle, controlled abstract paintings
Drysdale, Russell	1912-	Astringent, melancholy oil paintings of the Australian outback
Tucker, Albert	1914-	Paintings critical of modern urban life
Nolan, Sidney	1917-	Paintings devoted to themes of Australian folk mythology, the landscape of central Australia and the gold-rush era
Boyd, Arthur	1920-	Painter of naturalistic landscapes and of symbolic and mythical figures. Ceramic sculpture
Klippel, Robert	1920-	Delicate sculpture of great tension and control
Olsen, John	1928-	Paintings of industrial waterfront scenes and landscapes
Redpath, Norma	1928-	Abstract, powerful sculpture
Lanceley, Colin	1938-	Painter. Brightly colored collages and starkly linear paintings

FAMOUS NEW ZEALAND CULTURAL FIGURES AND THEIR PRINCIPAL WORKS

LITERATURE

Reeves, William Pember	1857-1932	Historian and intellectual leader of his generation: *The Long White Cloud*
Mackay, Jessie	1864-1938	Ballads and poems expressing a new national self-awareness: *The Spirit of Rangatira, The Sitter on the Rail*
Bethell, Mary Ursula	1874-1945	Intense evocations of landscape in poetry: *Collected Poems*
Mansfield, Katherine	1888-1923	Highly perfected, seemingly artless short stories, many of which have New Zealand settings: *The Short Stories of Katherine Mansfield, Journal of Katherine Mansfield*
Lee, John A.	1891-	Novels about the urban proletariat: *Children of the Poor*
Beaglehole, J. C.	1901-	Historian, essayist and poet
Holcroft, M. H.	1902-	Reflective literary and social criticism: *Discovered Isles*
Sargeson, Frank	1903-	Novels and short stories marked by penetrating social perception and effective reproduction of New Zealand speech patterns: *That Summer, I for One*
Fairburn, A. R. D.	1904-1957	Poet, essayist, journalist. One of New Zealand's few satirists and perhaps its most gifted love poet: *Strange Rendezvous, Three Poems*
Finlayson, Roderick	1904-	Stories about contemporary Maoris: *Brown Man's Burden, Sweet Beulah Land, The Schooner Came to Atia*
Mason, R. A. K.	1905-	Poems which brought New Zealand verse to a new standard of distinction: *No New Thing, This Dark Will Lighten*
Hyde, Robin	1906-1939	Poems re-creating the world of her youth: *Houses by the Sea.* Novels of social commentary, historical fiction and personal experience
McCormick, E. H.	1906-	Literary critic and biographer: *The Expatriate*
Brasch, Charles	1909-	Poet and founder and editor of *Landfall,* New Zealand's best literary periodical
Curnow, Allen	1911-	Influential poet, critic, anthologist and dramatist. Poems: *Island and Time, At Dead Low Water*
Glover, Denis	1912-	Poems sympathetic to the common man: *The Wind and the Sand, Arawata Bill*
Davin, Daniel Marcus	1913-	Novelist, short-story writer, war historian. Short stories: *The Gorse Blooms Pale*
Ashton-Warner, Sylvia	c.1918-	Novels characterizing emotionally disturbed women: *Spinster, Incense to Idols.* Essay: *Teacher*
Duggan, Maurice	1922-	Short stories: *Immanuel's Land*
Sinclair, Keith	1922-	Historian and poet
Ballantyne, David	1924-	Fictional study of a working-class family: *The Cunninghams*
Frame, Janet	1924-	Novels depicting emotionally unstable people: *Owls Do Cry, Faces in the Water, The Edge of the Alphabet, Scented Gardens for the Blind*
Cross, Ian	1925-	Novels: *The God Boy, After Anzac Day*
Baxter, James K.	1926-	Poet, critic and playwright. Perhaps the most gifted member of the postwar generation. Poems: *Beyond the Palisade; Blow, Wind of Fruitfulness; The Fallen House*
Shadbolt, Maurice	1932-	Short stories: *The New Zealanders, Summer Fires and Winter Country*

MUSIC

Lilburn, Douglas	1915-	Various compositions, including Symphony No. 1, the first symphony by a New Zealand composer

PAINTING AND SCULPTURE

Thompson, Sydney L.	1877-	Painter. Impressionist landscapes stressing light and color
McCormack, T. A.	1883-	Watercolor still lifes and landscapes, often influenced by Oriental art
Nicoll, Archibald F.	1886-	Landscapes and frankly realistic portraits
Weeks, John	1888-	Somber and subtly colored paintings and sketches in oil, chalk and watercolor
Page, Evelyn	1905-	Portraits and street scenes marked by a vigorous style
Hutton, John	1906-	Glass engravings for Britain's rebuilt Coventry Cathedral
Taylor, E. Mervyn	1906-	Wood engravings and watercolor paintings
Angus, Rita	1908-	Personal and imaginative landscapes. Portraits revealing a convincing image of the New Zealander
Lee-Johnson, Eric	1908-	Romantic landscapes of the rugged North Auckland countryside
Woollaston, M. T.	1910-	Low-keyed landscapes and portraits
Duff, Alison	1914-	Imaginative work in sculpture and other media, often employing bird and human forms
Macalister, Molly	1920-	Sculptor. Influenced in recent years by contemporary Italian sculpture
MacDairmid, Douglas	1922-	Landscapes expressing a deep feeling for the land

Credits

The sources for the illustrations in this book appear below. Credits for pictures from left to right are separated by commas, from top to bottom by dashes.

Cover—David Moore

8, 9—David Moore

10—Courtesy Government of Australia

11—Courtesy Government of New Zealand

12—Map by Rafael Palacios

14 through 21—David Moore

22—Derek Bayes courtesy Natural History Museum, London

25—Map by Rafael Palacios

29, 30, 31—David Moore

32, 33—George Silk

34, 35, 36—David Moore

45 through 57—David Moore

64 through 75—David Moore

81 through 85—David Moore

86, 87—George Silk

88 through 91—David Moore

98 through 105—David Moore

107—Australian News and Information Bureau Official Photograph by J. Band

111 through 119—David Moore

125—Tom Hutchins from Black Star for Sports Illustrated

126, 127, 128—John Dominis

129—Jerry Cooke

130, 131—David Moore for Sports Illustrated except top left; Fox Photos, top right; James Whitmore

132—Bob Gomel

139—David Moore

140—Radio Times Hulton Picture Library, David Moore

141—David Moore, Tom Hutchins from Black Star

142 through 145—David Moore

149, 150, 151—David Moore

ACKNOWLEDGMENTS

The editors wish to express their appreciation to Benjamin Haggott Beckhart, Professor Emeritus of Banking, Graduate School of Business, Columbia University, and former Visiting Professor at the Universities of Melbourne and Sydney, who read and commented on the entire text. The author is especially grateful to Ernest Shirley of the Time-Life News Service in Sydney, Australia, and Leslie Hobbs of Christchurch, New Zealand, for their valuable assistance to him in the preparation of the book.

Index

* This symbol in front of a page number indicates a photograph or painting of the subject mentioned.

Production staff for Time Incorporated

Arthur R. Murphy Jr. (Vice President and Director of Production)

Robert E. Foy, James P. Menton, Caroline Ferri and Robert E. Fraser

Text photocomposed under the direction of

Albert J. Dunn and Arthur J. Dunn

✕

Printed by R. R. Donnelley & Sons Company, Crawfordsville, Indiana

and The Safran Printing Company, Detroit, Michigan

Bound by R. R. Donnelley & Sons Company, Crawfordsville, Indiana

Paper by The Mead Corporation, Dayton, Ohio

Cover stock by The Plastic Coating Corporation, Holyoke, Massachusetts

INDIA
CEYLON
PHILIPPINES
MALAYSIA
INDONESIA
NEW GUINEA
PACIFIC
WESTERN SAMOA
INDIAN OCEAN
Tropic of Capricorn
AUSTRALIA
OCEAN
COOK IS. (N.Z.)
Darwin
Perth
SYDNEY
NEW ZEALAND
MELBOURNE
TASMANIA
Wellington
Equator
International Date Line
©RMcN.

TIMOR
DILI
ALOR
SELARU
K. VALSCH
WEST (Indon.)
ARAFURA SEA
TIMOR SEA
C. VAN DIEMEN
CROKER
COBOURG PEN.
MELVILLE
Van Diemen Gulf
CAPE ARNHEM
BATHURST
Clarence Str.
Darwin
GOVE PEN.
Blue Mud Bay
Anson Bay
Rum
Jungle
Pine Creek
ARNHEM LAND
GROOTE EYLANDT
CAPE LONDONDERRY
Joseph Bonaparte Gulf
Daly
Katherine
Roper
Limmen Bight
GUL OF CARPEN
SIR EDWARD PELLEW GROUP
Queens Chan.

INDIAN OCEAN

Collier Bay
Buccaneer Arch.
Wyndham
Mt. Hann 2800
Birdum
Daly Waters
Barroloola
Burke
CAPE LEVEQUE
Sunday Str.
KING LEOPOLD RANGES
Victoria River Downs
King Sd.
Derby
KIMBERLY
GEIKIE RANGE
Fitzroy Crossing
Halls Creek
Newcastle Waters
Broome
Roebuck Bay
Fitzroy
Ord
Woods
Alexandria
LaGrange
Stuart Cr.
Tanami
Tennant Creek
EIGHTY MILE BEACH
LARREY POINT
RIPON
DeGrey
Port Hedland
BARKLY TABLELAND
DAMPIER ARCH.
MONTE BELLO IS.
Roebourne
GREAT SANDY DESERT
Mackay
Barrow Creek
BARROW
Fortescue
Marble Bar
Mt. Ziel 4955
Arltunga
Hay
NORTH WEST CAPE
Millstream
Nullagine
MACDONNELL RANGES
Alice Springs
Exmouth Gulf
HAMERSLEY RANGE
Macdonald
JAMES RA.
Todd
SIMPSON
Onslow
Jiggalong
Ashburton
Mt. Bruce 4024
Amadeus
Disappointment
Mt. Olga 2600
Ayers Rock 2610
Finke
DESERT
POINT CLOATES
GIBSON DESERT
Mt. Woodroffe 4970
Charlotte Waters
Tropic of Capricorn
MUSGRAVE RANGES
CAPE FARQUHAR
Carnarvon
Peak Hill
Carnegie
Gillen
EVERARD RANGES
Oodnadatta
Gascoyne
Nabberu
The Alberga
BERNIER I.
Geographe Chan.
Wells
DORRE I.
Shark Bay
KIMBERLY RANGE
Wiluna
Eyre -39
DIRK HARTOG
Murchison
Meekatharra
Yeo
William Creek
STEEP POINT
Nannine
Coober Pedy
STUART RANGE
Cue
Sandstone
Laverton
Ajana
Austin
Mount Magnet
Carey
Farina
Northampton
Ballard
Raeside
GREAT VICTORIA DESERT
Torrens
HOUTMAN ROCKS
Menzies
Woomera
Parachil
Geraldton
Mingenew
Barlee
Oaldea Station
Everard
Pimba
Dongara
Moore
Hughes
Penong
Gairdner
Pithara
Kalgoorlie
Rawlinna
Ceduna
Whyalla
Miling
Lake Brown
Coolgardie
Goddards Soak
Eucla
Port Pirie
Moora
Boulder
NULLARBOR PLAIN
POINT FOWLER
Southern Cross
Lefroy
Eyre
EYRE PENINSULA
Moonta
SWANLAND
Cowan
Norseman
Swan
Northam
Dundas
GREAT AUSTRALIAN BIGHT
Perth
York
Salmon Gums
Port Lincoln
Adelaide
Fremantle
Gulf St. Vincent
Collie
Narrogin
Ravensthorpe
Esperance
KANGAROO
Geographe Bay
Bunbury
Hopetoun
Busselton
Katanning
ARCHIPELAGO OF THE RECHERCHE
CAPE NATURALISTE
DARLING RANGE
Enc
CAPE LEEUWIN
Nornalup
Albany
PT. D'ENTRECASTEAUX
WEST CAPE HOWE
King George Sd.

INDIAN OCEAN

110° Longitude East of Greenwich 115°